STAND THEREFORE

Discovering what it means to be a Christian Soldier

SCOTT A HARRISON
HPG Ministries
Pointing Souls to the Savior
Fort Worth, Texas

HPG Ministries
Fort Worth, TX 76131
www.hpgministries.com

ISBN 13: 9780989903714
ISBN: 0989903710
Scripture taken from the Holy Bible: King James Version
Stand Therefore was edited by Christian Author Services
www.christianbookeditor.com

Cover design by Adam Armstrong
www.sitegrafx.com

DEDICATION

This book is dedicated to my loving wife Lisa and children, who, through many years of moving from place to place, have stood by my side, supported, and loved me unconditionally.

I dedicate this book also to my mother and father, who through loving kindness took me to church when I was young and thereby introduced me to my Lord and Savior Jesus Christ without whom I would be lost and on my way to hell for all eternity. The peace and love of God is without respect and is available to whosoever will.

Romans 10:13

CALL TO DUTY

We are at war. This war began in the Garden of Eden and will end on a bloody battlefield in a place called Armageddon. The entire Bible is about this war. Satan is the enemy, and Christ has already won the victory. This book is not about Satan's attack on the world in general but rather about his attack on each of us as individual Christians in our role as individual soldiers in God's army. The time has come for all Christians to stand and fight — not a carnal war with rifles, bayonets, and hand grenades but a spiritual war.

In my lifetime I have seen the rapid decline of our great nation. War has reached our borders. As the United States of America, the last great hope for accomplishing Christ's Great Commission (Matthew 28:19-20) to evangelize the world falls to the wiles of the devil, most Christians stand on the sidelines despairing that anything can be done. We are to don the spiritual armor God has given us and fight that souls might be saved. Our Great Commander, the Lord Jesus Christ, died and rose again that we might have life and live a more abundant life. The Lord Jesus Christ paid the price for our sin before we realized we needed such a payment and by doing so, secured our salvation. Christ left with us the Holy Spirit by which we have the strength to stand. Having done all to stand, **stand therefore** (Ephesians 6:13-14).

Regardless of your circumstances or background, if you are saved by the blood of Jesus Christ, you are engaged in a spiritual war. This war is not being fought for land, wealth, or prosperity but rather for the souls of men and women. If we do not fight for those souls, who will? Jesus Christ, our Great Commander, has issued the orders (Mark 16:15; Ephesians 5:16). We are not called to be idle bystanders who sit on the sidelines critiquing others actively engaged in battle nor to mock those who have served and fallen. It is not our calling to criticize the lost world but rather to tell them of the good news that Jesus Lives! God forbid that we would ever look on those who have been over-run by the enemy and mock them. The scriptures tell us to come to the aid of those who are fallen and to lift those wounded in battle (Numbers 32:27). We have an enemy who never rests and will never give up and whose sole purpose is to destroy the soldiers of God and render them useless for the cause of Christ, which is that people may hear the gospel of Jesus Christ and be redeemed by His blood, shed on Calvary.

My bowels, my bowels! I am pained at my very heart; my heart maketh a noise in me; I cannot hold my peace, because thou hast heard, O my soul, the sound of the trumpet, the alarm of war.

- Jeremiah 4:19

INSPIRATION

During my time in the US Army, I discovered some great parallels between a Christian's life and that of a soldier. Though for many years I had entertained the thought of writing a book, and even had several false starts, I could never quite put the thoughts together for more than a few minutes at a time – until now. One day as I was sitting in my makeshift office staring at my dismal collection of books, my eyes happened upon the *Soldiers Manual of Common Tasks* I had kept from my time as a soldier. I thought to myself: Wouldn't it have been nice if I was issued a "common task" manual when I enlisted in the Lords' Army. As a private in the Lord's Army, I was not a great soldier. The "instruction" would have been very helpful to me. As I began thumbing through the table of contents of the *Soldiers Manual,* the Lord began revealing the parallels between the soldier life and the Christian life.

That is how the journey began in 2010. In this book I attempt to capture those parallels between the two and share some basic spiritual truths that every Christian, new and seasoned, should know before entering into battle. As you embark on this "basic training," my hope is that you will be strengthened and edified in both soul and spirit so as to march forward for Christ that souls may be saved.

Basic Training

The year was 1990. I was just 20 years old, struggling to make ends meet, and, unsure of God's will for my life, I took matters into my own hands and enlisted in the US Army. I was saved at the age of nine, and as a boy often marveled at the prospect of preaching and teaching the Word of God. I had no idea how to go about it and, honestly, I knew little or nothing even about being a Christian at the time. I mean, I knew what a Christian was but not how to be the Christian that God expected me to be. I was not alone. Sadly, most churches fail to provide believers with basic, fundamental Bible truths and fail to teach young Christians how to be soldiers for Christ. (This book is written for believers, so if by chance you are reading this book and you have never accepted Jesus Christ as your personal savior, please stop here and turn to the last chapter of this book, "How to be Saved," before reading on. It's the most important decision you will ever make.

Just as every soldier who enlists in any branch of service must go through basic military training, so you as a Christian must go through basic spiritual training. The purpose of basic training is to give you the fundamental knowledge and skills, the building blocks, for how to be a soldier for Christ. Though I will not attempt to teach you doctrine in this book, some doctrines may be revealed in the scriptural references quoted and in the last chapter on how to be saved. I will, however, share some basic Bible truths regarding salvation, eternal security for believers, and how to be an effective soldier for Jesus Christ. If you have ever served in the military, more than likely you have experienced some of the same things I will be discussing. Enjoy recounting the memories of your experience. If you have not served in the military, I will attempt to describe the experience as best I can.

Day One

May 22, 1990: I'm sitting in a hallway with 12 other young men, most of them about my age. We glance at one another, all trying to cloak the nervousness we are feeling inside. I remember distinctly saying to myself, "Self, what did you get yourself into?" We were all from different parts of Arizona gathered at the Phoenix MEPS (Military Entrance Processing Station). I did not know anyone in that corridor, but even so, we had something in common: In a few minutes all of us were going to raise our right hand and take an oath that would obligate us to service for the next few years. Four years for me, to be exact. Little did we know at the time that 72 days later Iraq would invade Kuwait and the United States of America would be engaged in a perpetual state of conflict with Iraq for the next 20 years.

A door opened and 12 young men came out of the room followed by two officers and a noncommissioned officer. Some were smiling and chatting among themselves, some had a blank stare on their faces. A sigh of relief fell on me until one of the officers, grinning slightly, said, "Last chance! After this, you're mine." The lump in my throat returned as we were escorted into the room. I was not nervous about serving. My father had served for 23 years, so I knew what to expect … sort of. I was nervous about making a four-year commitment. At the age of 20, four years is an eternity. They lined 12 of us in two rows, explained the procedure and that this was not to be taken lightly. They recited a few lines of the UCMJ (Uniform Code of Military Justice) regarding desertion (I recall glancing at the door and wondering if I should go for it) and the lack of freedom we would have for the duration of our commitment – all the while reminding us that we were *volunteering* for the service and could walk out now. Silence. Not one person in the room uttered a word or moved an inch. The officer told us to raise our right hand and repeat this oath:

> "I do solemnly swear (or affirm) that I will support and defend the Constitution of the United States against all enemies, foreign and domestic; that I will bear true faith and allegiance to the same; and that I will obey the orders of the President of the United States and the orders of the officers appointed over me, according to regulations and the Uniform Code of Military Justice. So help me God."

It was done. The oath was taken, the documents were signed. The door opened and we were led to the bedrooms where we would spend the last few hours of freedom before boarding a plane to basic training.

My father, a 20+ year veteran, gave me one simple piece of advice: "Keep your mouth shut and do what you're told." I would soon learn that this was the best advice anyone ever gave me. Upon our arrival at Ft. Leonard Wood, a seemingly nice staff sergeant picked up me and a few other soldiers and escorted us to the military installation. We were given some standard military briefings regarding regulations and uniforms and then filled out some paper-work. Two days into this journey we learned that we would be transferred to our barracks to complete our basic training. Judging from what I had seen thus far, this was going to be a breeze. I must admit, they had me fooled – hook, line, and sinker.

Day 3 started with 6 AM formation, chow, and packing our things for our move to the barracks. As we awaited our transportation, the staff sergeant gushed on about how wonderful the training would be and even told us that we were moving to the nicest barracks on the post. I was expecting a tour bus to pull up to take us to our new luxury villa, so my countenance fell when the cattle truck rumbled up. It was a simple tractor trailer contraption that looked like a modified horse trailer. If you haven't had the distinct pleasure of enjoy-ing this experience, just imagine being stuffed into a horse trailer with 30 or so soldiers in the May heat of Missouri. Lovely!

As we boarded the cattle truck in my mind I heard cow bells ringing as I was shoved to the back by all the men scrambling to climb aboard. Before we could get settled, the truck started rolling, tossing us around like bowling pins. There is a reason they call this state *Misery!* No offense to those from the Show Me state, but it was scorching hot and sticky and we did not see much air conditioning for the next eight weeks. We drove around post for what seemed like an hour. The heat was almost unbearable. The sweat running down my face and into my eyes made it hard to see. As every minute passed, the anticipation rose. Through the burning sensation in my eyes, I could only catch glimpses of the road and buildings ahead. I didn't know what I was looking for anyway but that did not stop me from looking. I was getting nervous. Looking around, I notice some of the other young men and they were scared stiff. Others looked anxious. Some simply stared blankly out the holes in side of the trailer. We pulled up to what seemed to be a very nice, newly built, set of barracks. Six drill sergeants were standing out front to greet us, all with big smiles on their faces. I recall thinking to myself that, except for the cattle truck ride in the scorching heat, this was not as bad as my brother and father had told me it was going to be.

Just then a drill sergeant stepped onto the cattle car. He looked us up and down, took a deep breath, and started screaming at the top of his lungs: "You've got five seconds to get your tails off this truck!" Needless to say he chose more colorful words to express himself, so colorful that I will spare you the details. I cannot describe the sheer pain and agony we endured over the next four hours, picking up and putting down the 75-pound duffle bags we had with us. We did get occasional breaks from the duffle bag duty – breaks to do endless push-ups, flutter kicks, and various other exercises designed to inflict on us as much pain as possible in the least amount of time. All the while the drill sergeant was screaming in our ears, so close that my ear was wet with his spit. Twenty years later I can still hear the screaming and yelling and remember the pain.

The next eight weeks was more of the same. My name was replaced with "Private." I was not even given the courtesy of a last name, although it was written on my hat. By Week 7, I had run more miles than I had driven a car to that point in my life and marched more miles in than I had walked. It was only then that I began to understand what was taking place and why we were treated that way. They were breaking us down so that we would forget about "I" as individuals and begin to see "us" as a unit. Everything we did was aimed at building a team of men who would work together towards one common goal. This is where we begin our journey and begin to draw parallels between Basic Training and the Word of God.

Endure Hardness

Although the Bible gives few instructions to real soldiers, it draws a parallel to which we should pay close attention. The Bible tells us in 2 Timothy 2:3 to "endure hardness." "*Thou therefore endure hardness, as a good soldier of Jesus Christ.*" Verse 4 adds, "*No man that warreth entangleth himself with the affairs of this life; that he may please him who hath chosen him to be a soldier.*" The purpose of those long days spent marching mile after mile, the morning runs and exercises to build our strength and endurance, was so that when we were faced with a similar situation in battle, we would endure hardness and pull through to victory. This endurance is not just for your own sake as a soldier. Remember, we are not fighting this battle alone; but we are part of the Lord's army. There are others by our side who look to us to gain strength and will suffer as well if we stumble, fall by the wayside, or give up. So we should endure hardness for others as well as for ourselves. Do not take it lightly that God has called you to be a soldier. Many of the trials and tribulations we face are to prepare us for the battle. Some such trials are themselves the battle and require us to stand strong in the Lord and the power of His might so "*that ye may be able to withstand in the evil day, and having done all to stand. Stand therefore*" (Ephesians 6:13-14).

Secondly, the lesson we were to learn from this experience was that we are not our own. We were to be a unit and fight as a team. We all bore personal responsibility to take care of ourselves, but when it came to battle, we were trained to fight and move as one single unit. We always had a "battle buddy" as they called it. Our battle buddy was someone to watch our back and hold us accountable for our actions. My battle buddy kept me out of trouble more than once. 1 Corinthians 6:19-20 says, "*What? Know ye not that your body is the temple of the Holy Ghost which is in you, which ye have of God, and ye are not your own? For ye are bought with a price.*"

The whole purpose of the seemingly chaotic first four weeks of training was to accomplish these two purposes. The hardness we had to endure was to take us to a place where we no longer thought as individuals but as a unit. It was to replace our natural self-centeredness with an orientation toward others so that we were no longer concerned with our own individual needs but with the needs of those around us – those whom God has chosen to be with us in battle. 1 Corinthians 12:12 says, "*For as the body is one, and hath many members, and all the members of that one body, being many, are one body; so also in Christ.*"

We were broken down to be built back up again. In John 12:12 Jesus said, "*Verily, verily, I say unto you, Except a grain of wheat falls into the ground and dies, it abides alone: but if it dies, it brings forth much fruit.*" In order for us to do anything for the Lord, we, like the seed or the box containing precious ointment, must be broken in body, soul, and spirit. Only then can Christ be revealed in us. In addition, we cannot win the battle on our own. Have you ever seen a battle being fought by one soldier? It takes a concerted, team effort. We must work together with our fellow believers to accomplish the will and work of our Lord and Savior Jesus Christ. Christ Himself gathered together to Himself 12 men to take the gospel first to Israel and then to the entire world.

How much more then should we bind together for the cause of Christ (Hebrews 10:25)? In order to do so, we must first take our Lord's basic training course. I am not talking about four years of college or eight weeks of intensive exercise but rather about taking the time to recognize and understand what Christ expects from us and what we need to do to prepare for battle.

In Week 3 of our training, we received the *Soldier's Manual of Common Tasks*, skill level 1. This served as our guide for the next few weeks. It detailed the many skills we were required to learn before graduating from basic training. It contained everything a soldier needed to know to go to battle. Would to God that all believers would put themselves through such a test to ensure proficiency with some basic skills before stepping onto the spiritual battlefield. Doing so would save many lives and result in far fewer casualties. While I do not claim that this book contains everything you need to know about being a soldier for Christ, I do pray that it will serve as a guide to help you along the way. My sincerest hope is that you can draw strength and develop the skills and knowledge needed to be an effective soldier for Christ. One thing is for certain: Knowing everything *about* the Bible will not help you. Knowing the Christ of the scriptures will do more for you than all the knowledge in the world (John 5:39)

"GOD IS RECRUITING SOLDIERS TO FIGHT IN THE BATTLE. WAR IS AT THE GATES. SOLDIERS ARE NEEDED TO PROCLAIM THE TRUTH THAT SOULS MAY BE SAVED."   - Unknown

---

1

PURPOSE

I have given a lot of thought to my days as a soldier and the years following after I gave my life to the Lord. As I grew in the Lord and learned more about the Bible, I was amazed at the parallels between my experience as a soldier in the US Army and my experience as a soldier in God's Army of born-again believers who are engaged in a great spiritual battle. The objective of this book is three-fold:

(1) to help Christians recognize that all Christians who are saved by the grace of God (and not "Christians" in name only) are engaged in the same fight.

(2) to equip Christians to become victorious on the field of battle.

(3) to inspire Christians not merely to *say* we are soldiers for Christ but to actually enter the fight and prevail against the enemy in leading souls to our Lord that He may save them from an eternity in hell.

To meet these objectives, all Christians need to be equipped and trained via some fundamental guidelines for becoming effective soldiers for Christ.

We take our purpose statement from the Army's *Soldier's Manual of Common Tasks: According to STP 21-1-SMCT*:

> "Training prepares soldiers, leaders, and units to fight and win in combat.... The Soldier's Manual of Common Tasks (SMCT), Skill Level (SL) 1, contains the common tasks that are essential to the Army's ability to win on the modern battlefield. In the event of war, regardless of job or individual MOS, each soldier risks exposure to hostile actions. This manual contains the standardized training objectives for the common tasks which will help soldiers fight, survive, and win in combat."

As Christian soldiers we, too, have a manual – the Bible, God's word – that provides us with our purpose statement. Here we find our text in Ephesians 6:10-18:

> "Finally, my brethren, be strong in the Lord, and in the power of his might. Put on the whole armour of God, that ye may be able to stand against the wiles of the devil. For we wrestle not against flesh and blood, but against principalities, against powers, against the rulers of the darkness of this world, against spiritual wickedness in high places. Wherefore take unto you the whole armour of God, that ye may be able to withstand in the evil day, and having done all, to stand. Stand therefore...."

Understandably, a great many books, sermons, and commentaries have been written on this passage of scripture and rightfully so. An ill-prepared soldier will quickly become a hindrance to the battle or a casualty. The modern-day soldier spends three times the effort in training as he does in actual combat. This extensive training is essential not only to the survival of the individual soldier but to the survival of those in his unit with whom he serves. *Having the necessary training and equipment is critical.*

Think about how the importance of training, preparation, and equipment applies to many endeavors. Would those who hunt for a living go out after big game without a rifle? Would he not have first scoped out the terrain and prepared for the trip? Take sports. Would a football player step on to a football field without the necessary protective gear? Would a baseball player step up to home plate without a batting helmet and a bat? Of course not. Can you imagine a soldier showing up to guard duty without a weapon to defend the fort? What good would he be? That would be ludicrous. Be prepared! Yet how many of us walk out of our houses each day and onto the spiritual battlefield of the Christian life having spent not one minute in preparation with our Lord?

We are at war! Prepare yourself for the battle, soldier! The war will not stop because you have not the time or inclination to prepare. The battle will rage on. You will simply become a casualty and thereby distract another soldier from defending the stronghold or advancing on the enemy because he must stop to take care of you. Although it is not written in any military manual I know of, it goes without saying that we do not leave our fellow soldiers on the field of battle when they are wounded. Don't be a distraction to other Christians by becoming a casualty. PREPARE YOURSELF each and every day, several times a day if necessary so that "HAVING DONE ALL" you can "STAND. STAND THEREFORE." Put on the whole armor of God, not just *some* of it. Don't put on the helmet and leave off the breastplate, or take up the shield and forget about the belt! And take your sword with you when you go. Be prepared!

Throughout the Old Testament we find soldiers preparing for war. Unfortunately, most Christians today do not prepare for battle and most never enter into battle. The Old Testament provides us with many great examples of the life of a soldier. David, who was a type of Christ in the Old Testament, was also a great model for Christian soldiers, especially in the early years of his calling. The way David handled certain situations in his early years helps us understand our role as soldiers of Christ.

David was neither the Hebrew people's nor Samuel's first choice. We see that Samuel himself looked to Jesse's oldest son Eliab (David's oldest brother) first when God sent him to anoint a new king. We read in 1 Samuel 16:6: "*And it came to pass, when they were come, that he looked on Eliab, and said, Surely the*

LORDS's *anointed is before him.*" Eliab was likely a comely man of great stature who by birthright held the favored position in the family. In 1 Samuel 16:7, however, God interjects to correct Samuel, and this verse marks the beginning of a theme that carries throughout the rest of the scriptures: God looks *not* on the outward appearance but on the heart of a man. 1 Samuel 16:7 says, *"But the LORD said unto Samuel, Look not on his countenance, or on the height of his stature; because I have refused him: for the LORD seeth not as man seeth; for man looketh on the outward appearance, but the LORD looketh on the heart."*

A Heart Right with God

This means that in order to answer the call to duty, we must have a heart that is right with God. Many soldiers enter the battle with an unprepared heart that is not right with God. The devil, that old serpent, makes quick work of those soldiers who enter the battlefield in the flesh. Even those whom God has blessed with fair speech, a comely appearance, and great knowledge about the Bible have fallen or become casualties whom others must then care for or nurture when they entered the field of battle relying on their outward abilities. God is not interested in your ability to fight in the flesh. God is interested in your willingness to be obedient. God is interested in your heart.

The Lord has humbled me on many occasions when I thought I could stand in my own power. Every time I enter the field of battle without preparing my heart before God, the results are always the same – *disastrous*. Those who do not prepare before going into battle do not last the day. They are rendered useless for the cause and are living a defeated life. Though we all stumble and fall on occasion, we must get back up and press forward. The enemy will not retreat unless we press on (James 4:7).

To be victorious in battle, we must follow the instructions Christ has laid out for us. We cannot expect to win the war for Christ if we fail to follow even the simplest instructions. We can be victorious *if* we obey and discipline ourselves to endure hardship and stand when the enemy is at the gates.

Before being deployed to Operation Desert Storm, our unit spent count-less hours training and retraining in basic soldiering skills. Since I was fresh out of basic training the tasks were still familiar to me. I recall seeing other soldiers and Non-Commissioned Officers struggling with some of the most basic tasks. If we do not continue to train and stay proficient in the basic skills we are supposed to know, we will lose the ability to react appropriately when the time comes. 1 Timothy 5:13 says, "*And withal they learn to be idle, wandering about from house to house; and not only idle, but tattlers also and busybodies, speaking things which they ought not.*" An idle mind and idle hands are a breeding ground for sin. The enemy stands ready to pounce and distract you from doing the work of God if he senses any lack of preparedness.

Thus we absolutely *must* prepare ourselves and be diligent in the work of the Lord. Just as in the US Army not every soldier is an infantryman nor a commander. Regardless of what God has called you to do, be diligent in the task. I have known many a prayer warrior who never had the opportunity to witness with a lost soul face-to-face. But I know that without that prayer war-rior's prayers, those who go out and search the highways and hedges for the lost would not last the day. The US Army is not made up only of foot soldiers. For the military to fight successfully many different jobs must be performed. Without that support, the troops in the field would go without food, water, medical supplies, ammo, fuel, and much more. One thing is certain, though: All who perform these functions are soldiers, and *all* soldiers must be as pre-pared as if they were fighting on the front line.

2

CHARACTERISTICS

The life of a soldier is one that few can understand. Soldiers are a special breed of persons who have voluntarily put aside all their freedoms in order to defend others' right to express theirs. A soldier's life is filled with loneliness because he or she must be separated from loved ones – spouse, children, parents, siblings, and friends – for days, weeks, and, recently, even years on end. Within a soldier there abides great strength and devotion to duty that far surpasses that of ordinary citizens. I can recall being in the deserts of Iraq, the hills of Colorado, and the backwoods of Kentucky counting down the hours until I could return home to loved ones. Make no mistake: I did not despise my duty. Not at all. Rather I stood proud that I could serve the country I love and defend her freedoms. But still I longed to be home with those I hold closest to my heart.

Qualities of an Effective Soldier

To be a soldier one needs to have certain qualities. Fortunately these qualities can be learned, and we Christian Soldiers would do well to learn them quickly.

A soldier is where he ought to be. Punctuality and timeliness are traits of every true soldier. When the call to battle is given, he is there. When he is not in battle, he is training (reading and studying), checking his gear (praise and worship), and preparing for the battle (prayer).

Take David, for example. David was where he was supposed to be (with one exception). After Samuel had all Jesse's sons pass before him, he was a little confused because the Lord had not chosen any of them. 1 Samuel 16:11 says, "And Samuel said unto Jesse, Are here all thy children? And he said, There remaineth yet the youngest, and, behold, he keepeth the sheep. And Samuel said unto Jesse, Send and fetch him: for we will not sit down till he come hither." David was right where he was supposed to be when God called him into service.

As we were preparing to go to Iraq, one soldier in our unit in particular could not wait to go. He was so excited about going and getting into the fight. Ironically, however, he never saw the battle. I was told he injured himself while dancing on a table at a bar before the war started and never saw a single day of combat. In Matthew 22:14 Jesus said, "For many are called, but few are chosen." God has called us to be soldiers. God has called us to the battle. Our part is to be about the Lord's work, being where we ought to be, and having our heart right with God so that when the time comes for us to enter the fight we are ready to serve.

<u>A soldier knows how to use his weapons and use them skill-fully</u>. 2 Timothy 2:15 instructs us to "study to shew thyself approved unto God, a workman that needeth not to be ashamed, rightly dividing the word of truth." Though I devote an entire chapter (chapter 10) to the weapons and armor of a Christian soldier, I want to take a moment here to mention that a soldier has many weapons at his disposal and that a true soldier of Christ knows how and when to use each and every one. Every soldier must use discernment and discretion. If he uses the wrong weapon at the wrong time, it is likely he will do more harm than good. Some weapons are for offensive purposes and some for defensive ones. To achieve success in battle – meaning winning souls for Christ – we must defend the fort from the enemy's attacks and advance on the field of battle. The right weapon for the job means that there is no need to use a grenade when a properly placed shot from a sidearm will do.

We have the Word of God. Hebrews 4:12 tells us that "the word of God is quick, and powerful, and sharper than any two-edged sword, piercing even to the dividing asunder of soul and spirit, and of the joints and marrow, and is a discerner of the thoughts and intents of the heart." We will discuss this in much greater detail in Chapter 10.

We have our Testimony. 2 Corinthians 1:12 says, "For our rejoicing is this, the testimony of our conscience, that in simplicity and godly sincerity, not with fleshly wisdom, but by the grace of God, we have had our conversation in the world, and more abundantly to you-ward."

I stand amazed at how the Lord works in our lives as Christians and soldiers for the cross. Once we have our heart right with God and are about the Father's business, He calls us to service and gives us a good testimony. As we continue examining David's life in 1 Samuel 16, we see that only five verses after Samuel asked Jesse to fetch his youngest son and God anointed him as the one who would succeed Saul, God called David out of the pasture where he was tending the sheep. Note that David went right back to tending the sheep after being anointed the new king over God's people. We should be humble and not think more highly of ourselves than we ought (Romans 12:3).

Look again at 1 Samuel 16:18-19. After the Lord troubled Saul and he needed some music to soothe his troubled spirit, "Then answered one of the servants, and said, Behold, I have seen a son of Jesse the Bethlehemite, that is cunning in playing, and a mighty valiant man, and a man of war, and prudent in matters, and a comely person, and the LORD is with him. Wherefore Saul sent messengers unto Jesse, and said, Send me David thy son, which is with the sheep." Now how in the world did this servant find out about David and know that David was all these things? How did David get such a testimony? He was just a lad at the time. That is the power of God. The change that takes place in a person when he submits his life wholly and truly to God and the service of the Lord Jesus Christ is truly miraculous.

I recall being in the motor pool at Fort Knox, Kentucky, when a fellow soldier made an unsavory comment and told an off-color joke. He turned to me and apologized and said, "Sorry, preacher, I didn't know you were there. You don't know anything about *that*, now do you?" First, I wasn't a preacher at the time, though I was honored he bestowed such a prestigious title on me. Second, I realized that God had given me a testimony before those soldiers so that they actually thought I had never done anything wrong in my entire life! PRAISE GOD!!! If they only knew how deep and dark was that pit that God pulled me out of when He saved my wretched soul.... But I'm glad they didn't. Psalm 40:2 says, "He brought me up also out of an horrible pit, out of the miry clay, and set my feet upon a rock, *and* established my goings." He gave me a new beginning when He saved me. 2 Corinthians 5:17 says, "Therefore if any man be in Christ, he is a new creature: old things are passed away; behold, all things are become new."

We have our Family. Psalm 127:3-5 says, "Lo, children are an heritage of the LORD: and the fruit of the womb is his reward. As arrows are in the hand of a mighty man; so are children of the youth. Happy is the man that hath his quiver full of them: they shall not be ashamed, but they shall speak with the enemies in the gate." Although there is much to say about children and childrearing, I have neither the time nor the expertise to deal with the subject here. I will say, however, that my wife Lisa and I never tired of hearing folks tell us what well-behaved children when we were dining out in restaurants or at the market. We have truly been blessed with good Godly children.

That is not to say that we have not gone through the pains of parenthood, and as for those teenage years, well, I will say this: My entire perspective changed after our children went through their teen years, and I was not so judgmental of others after witnessing my own children, whom we had raised, seem to challenge us at every turn. Take heart, if you are parenting a teen, for they come back around about 18 or so. God knew this, and if we read Proverbs 22:6 carefully we note that there is a colon between "Train up a child in the way he should go" and "and when he is old, he will not depart from it." The colon in this verse is the gap I call the "dark years." Depending on the child the dark years occur sometime between the ages of 12–19. It is during these years that their true character is formed. I cannot stress enough the importance of submerging them in the Word of God and in a good church with Godly influences.

A soldier knows how to carry heavy loads without complaining. 2 Timothy 2:3 says, "Thou therefore endure hardness, as a good soldier of Jesus Christ." Soldiers must sometimes carry heavy burdens and sometimes they must carry other soldiers. Herein lies a great truth that many Christians fail to understand. Many believers struggle with a subtle form of pride, the root sin of the wicked one, that makes us rather see the fallen soldier fall even farther. Why? Because deep down in that part of our heart that is not yet submitted to Christ, we are elevated in stature and glorify ourselves in our own eyes and in those we are closest to. The timed response and phony sorrowful cluck of our tongues as we utter the words, "it is so sad what happened to Brother or Sister _____ ." You fill in the blank. Lord, forgive us for not lifting the burden off of our fellow comrades in the faith and picking them up when they have fallen.

During basic training and other training exercises we would go on road marches. Every soldier was required to bring the necessary equipment with him in his rucksack, weighing *at least* 50 pounds along with his weapon. Trust me, they weighed them. If our rucksack didn't weigh at least 50 pounds, we got a special surprise – rocks in the rucksack. We carried other essentials that the unit shared, including a few M60 machine guns and usually at least one PRC-77 radio, and our unit's flag. No one, and I mean *no one*, wanted to carry the extra load of the machine gun or the radio. It was difficult to carry the extra weight while maintaining your position in the ranks. More often than not, the sergeant in charge would designate the largest soldier to carry the extra load, which was pretty unfortunate for me. Being 6' 2" and weighing about 220, I often had the privilege of carrying the machine gun or the radio, and sometimes both. It took everything I had, physically and mentally, to carry those loads without complaining.

The Lord often looks to the strong in faith to bear the load of those who are not. Galatians 6:2 says, "Bear ye one another's burdens, and so fulfill the law of Christ." Christ Himself bore our burdens all the way to the cross. He bears our burdens now when we need help. I have never ever gone to the Lord for help and been turned away. I do have to say, though, that most of the burdens we Christians carry are self-imposed, spiritual and carnal.

A soldier trains daily for the battle. Ephesians 6:18 says, "Praying always with all prayer and supplication in the Spirit, and watching thereunto with all perseverance and supplication for all saints." Chapter 4: Training Tips covers the topic of prayer in detail. But know this: A soldier trains each and every day for what is inevitably coming – **war**. In our nation's 237-year history, we have enjoyed only a few years of true peace. When I joined the Army in May, 1990, the thought of going to war had not entered into my mind. I was sorely mistaken because before I had even finished my training the conflict in Iraq had started. As Christians, we should not be caught unaware. The battle is just around the corner.

Yes, we have our place, our sanctuary, where we gather strength and prepare for the battle, but the battle rages on in our minds from the moment we wake up in the morning till our head hits the pillow at night. If the battle is not always physical, there is a constant battle raging in our minds. Our prayer should be that of David who prayed in 1 Chronicles 29:18, "O LORD God of Abraham, Isaac, and of Israel, our fathers, keep this forever in the imagination of the thoughts of the heart of thy people, and prepare their heart unto thee." Prepare yourself and pray that God will keep both your heart and your thoughts pure.

A soldier obeys orders from the commander. In John 10:27 Jesus said, "My sheep hear my voice, and I know them, and they follow me." Obedience is without dispute. We must be obedient to our Lord and Savior Jesus Christ. Soldiers in the Army are not to question the orders of the commander but only to obey them. We are required to obey even when we do not understand the order. Many times in my Christian life I have wondered why the Lord wanted me to do certain things. I would be lying if I said that I have always obeyed the Lord in everything He has asked of me. As I look back on the things I questioned, I can now see that the Lord's hand was in it. While I did not understand at the time, I now know that it was for my own good or the good of my family.

Perhaps the second greatest example of obedience given to us in the scriptures (the first, of course, being Christ on the cross) is that of Abraham when the Lord asked him to sacrifice his son Isaac (Genesis 22:1-14). These passages are a picture of what our Lord Jesus Christ would do on the cross so that we might have eternal life. God asked Abraham to sacrifice his beloved son not only as a measure of his obedience, but so that he would understand that nothing should come between his relationship with his Lord and Savior. In the short time that his son Isaac was alive, Abraham had elevated him to a position in his heart above the Lord. In these few passages we see both Abraham's obedience and God's mercy working in an unimaginable way.

A soldier keeps his uniform spotless. Psalm 119:9 says, "wherewithal shall a young man cleanse his way? by taking heed thereto according to thy word. With my whole heart have I sought thee: O let me not wander from thy commandments. Thy word have I hid in mine heart, that I might not sin against thee." Revelation 16:15 says, "Behold, I come as a thief. Blessed *is* he that watcheth, and keepeth his garments, lest he walk naked, and they see his shame." Ephesians 5:27 says, "That he might present it to himself a glorious church, not having spot, or wrinkle, or any such thing; but that it should be holy and without blemish."

A soldier knows how to fight on different battlefields. A skilled soldier knows how to fight on various battlefields —on a mountain range, down in the valley, and in the dry heat of the desert. (For more on this topic, see Chapter 8.)

3

SOLDIER'S RESPONSIBILITY

I n almost every building on every US military installation around the world, you will find a wall hung with photographs of those in the chain of command. The chain of command extends all the way up to the Commander in Chief, who is the President of the United States. Farther down, the chain splits into branches for each service, and then further divides for local command, and finally drops down to the individual soldier himself. The chain of command is personal for every soldier and is not simply some random hierarchy of personnel in the Army. Every soldier, airman, sailor, or marine has a chain of command. The chain of command is to be followed both down the line (when orders are given or passed down) and up the line (for reporting and accountability). The integrity of the chain of command is without compromise. A soldier is responsible for knowing the chain of command from the Commander in Chief to the lowest ranking soldier in his unit.

Likewise, every Christian soldier has a chain of command. God the Father is the Commander in Chief, Jesus Christ our Lord is the Great General, and the Holy Spirit is the Ambassador of our Faith. Of course, because each Person of the triune Godhead is co-equal, we could attribute each member of the Godhead to any of these roles, but for illustration purposes these will suffice. The chain of command continues down to our Pastor as the captain of the company and then to Deacons, teachers, and church leaders as the officers over the troops. We even have unnamed persons in our churches who have been appointed to informal leadership positions. We will call such persons "the mighty men." These men and women stand head and shoulders above the rest (spiritually speaking) because they have learned what it is to live a "crucified" life. The "crucified" life is evident in their speech, their demeanor, and their testimony.

True soldiers of Christ will respect the authority of those appointed over them and accept their position in the church (Philippians 2:3). Each one of us has three primary responsibilities – to God, to family, and to our local church. I believe most would agree that they *must* fall in this order.

The Christian's Responsibility to God

God requires obedience rather than sacrifice. 1 Samuel 15:22-23 says, "And Samuel said, Hath the LORD *as great* delight in burnt offerings and sacrifices, as in obeying the voice of the LORD? Behold, to obey *is* better than sacrifice, *and* to hearken than the fat of rams. For rebellion *is as* the sin of witchcraft, and stubbornness *is as* iniquity and idolatry. Because thou hast rejected the word of the LORD, he hath also rejected thee from *being* king."

To be a soldier is to be obedient. Soldiers are taught to obey orders without asking questions. This was another lesson I learned early in my eight weeks of training. As I mentioned earlier, my father gave me a particular bit of advice before I left for basic training that I remember to this day. His advice was: "Keep your mouth shut and do what you're told." Well, in Week 5 of basic training I was reprimanded for being on the wrong floor of the barracks after lights out. I informed the drill sergeant that I was in fact on the correct floor and that I had been a part of his squad since day one. Here's a word to the wise: Never correct a drill sergeant, even if he is wrong. Though he was a little embarrassed over the fact that he did not recognize me, he did not hesitate to make me do pushups anyway. The drill sergeants had focused all of their attention on those soldiers who were not obedient and thus had to be reprimanded constantly and simply forgotten about me because I was following my father's advice. God blessed my obedience by making my time in training a little easier than some others'.

We Christians have the perfect example of this obedience in the scriptures – Christ Himself who became obedient to the cross when He did not have to do so. Philippians 2:3-8, tells us:

> "Let nothing be done through strife or vainglory; but in lowliness of mind let each esteem other better than themselves. Look not every man on his own things, but every man also on the things of others. Let this mind be in you, which was also in Christ Jesus: Who, being in the form of God, thought it not robbery to be equal with God: But made himself of no reputation, and took upon him the form of a servant, and was made in the likeness of men: And being found in fashion as a man, he humbled himself, and became obedient unto death, even the death of the cross."

If Christ Himself can be obedient and make Himself of no reputation we who are empowered by the Holy Spirit can certainly do the same.

To be obedient is to submit to authority. That is, the authority of those *over* us. When we do so, we glorify Christ. To be a Christian is to be Christ-like. Many call themselves Christians and rebel against every authority. I count myself fortunate to have been a member of several churches whose senior pastors were held in such high regard that I never heard one cross word about them. I know from the testimony of others that this is not the case in every church.

In most cases, we Christians have a choice when it comes to selecting a church and a pastor to follow. I say "in most cases" because this has not always been so for me personally. God has taken me to churches to which I was certain I did not belong in order to teach me to submit to authority. I would be lying if I told you that it was an easy lesson to learn or that I did not struggle with God regarding this matter. Fortunately, I had let God take control and He has blessed my family and me beyond measure.

A rebellious spirit is that nature that needs to be in submission to God and is often the most difficult to yield. To rebel is to be like that wicked one, the devil, who was the first to rebel against the authority of God (Isaiah 14:13).

But you and I are not to be rebellious. The root sin of rebellion is pride (Proverbs 29:23). Pride is the sin, and rebellion is the manifestation of pride. Christ provides us with the perfect example of what we ought to be and how we ought to think. Romans 12:3 says, "For I say, through the grace given unto me, to every man that is among you, not to think of himself more highly than he ought to think; but to think soberly, according as God hath dealt to every man the measure of faith." Our relationship with God must be right before our relationships with our family or church family will be right.

Glorify His Son

Every Christian has a responsibility to glorify Christ. We must live our lives knowing that everyone is watching what we say and do. So how do we glorify Christ? We glorify Christ by being obedient to His will and by holding Him in higher regard than we hold ourselves. Jesus Himself said in Matthew 5:16, "Let your light so shine before men, that they may see your good works, and glorify your Father which is in heaven." Secondly, we glorify Christ when we hold others in higher regard than we hold ourselves. Philippians 2:3 tells us to "let nothing be done through strife or vainglory; but in lowliness of mind let each esteem other better than themselves." This is the exact opposite of what the world teaches us. The world teaches us to look out for ourselves first and others only after all of our needs are met. I have heard many times in my career a saying that may be familiar to you. Most people are tuned in to the station WIIFM: *What's In It For Me?* Romans 1:22 says, "Professing themselves to be wise, they became fools."

As soldiers for Christ we need to put off the old man and put on the new. 2 Corinthians 5:17 tells us: "Therefore if any man be in Christ, he is a new creature: old things are passed away; behold, all things are become new." To *say* you are a Christian is one thing; to live the life of a Christian is another. I often ask my Sunday School class the following question: "Would those you are around every day know you were a Christian if you did not tell them?"

Think about that for a moment. Does your life speak to others? Do your actions portray Christ? Jesus said, "By their fruits ye shall know them"

(Matthew 7:20), and James tells us, "For as the body without the spirit is dead, so faith without works is dead also" (James 2:26). Our calling is to glorify Christ in word and deed so that others may know that what you have is real salvation and not just religion. The Bible gives us an example of what it is to glorify Christ in Psalms 19:1: "The heavens declare the glory of God...." Now think about that for a moment. The heavens declare the glory of God. We see the heavens only at night, and what do we see when we look towards the heavens? We see the stars shining in a dark place and the moon reflecting the light of the sun (Son). So we glorify Christ when we reflect His light and shine as a star in a dark place (John 3:35).

The Christian's Responsibility to Family

Responsibility to family means being responsible to those whom God has given to us – to our spouse first, our children second, and our other family members third. Many get the order of responsibility jumbled up, which causes great trouble in the home and is a recipe for marital and family dysfunction.

Marriage: Husbands and Wives

Many a husband esteems his mother above his own wife. Brother, this ought not to be so. Don't misunderstand me. We are always to honor our parents and give them the respect they are due, but when a man and woman enter into the bond of marriage this union and relationship ought to come first. Echoing God's command when He instituted the very first marriage, Ephesians 5:30 states, "For this cause shall a man leave his father and mother, and shall be joined unto his wife, and they two shall be one flesh." By the same token, a wife should not esteem her father more highly than her husband. And husbands and wives should *never* dare compare each other with their parents. The unity of marriage is a sacred unity established and blessed by God.

Parent-Child Relationship

Your children are precious gifts from God, but your relationship with them should be placed in a position beneath that of your relationship with your spouse. I have seen many a marriage suffer because husbands and wives put their children first in the home – above each other. This is not to say that we are to neglect our children. God forbid. It is to say that we are called to honor our spouse first and meet their needs before our children's needs. This is completely contrary to what the world teaches us. But remember that we are not of this world but are to separate ourselves from the world. 1 Corinthians 3:19 says, "For the wisdom of this world is foolishness with God. For it is written, He taketh the wise in their own craftiness."

The greatest gift we can give our children is to show them true love, selfless love, and a bond of unity that mirrors the relationship between Christ and His church. Ephesians 5:25 provides us with the model: "Husbands, love your wives, even as Christ also loved the church, and gave himself for it." If we raise our children in the love and admonition of the Lord, we will teach them to honor God first and live by this example in our marriage. Then, when they are old they will not depart from the Lord and His will for their lives. Proverbs 22:6 says, "Train up a child in the way he should go: and when he is old, he will not depart from it."

Men, be very careful not to sacrifice your family for the work of the Lord. Our Lord would not have it so. If God calls you into His service in any capacity, He will also call your family. Rarely has God called men to service that has broken a home. God established your marriage and will not see it destroyed. To destroy the bond of marriage is to destroy the picture of Christ and the church. If by chance you were saved after marrying and your spouse is not yet saved, your primary responsibility is to see to it that he or she is saved. That is your main mission field. If you are single, see to it that you find a mate who is saved. The Bible clearly states that we believers should not be unevenly yoked together with unbelievers (2 Corinthians 6:14).

Far too many believers take their families for granted. Sadly, I have seen the homes of pastors and missionaries broken because they neglected to take care of their own family in the way that God intended. A family that serves God together has a great testimony before a lost world. As the old adage goes, "a family that prays together, stays together." I cannot tell you the origin of that saying, but it is certainly true. Setting aside family time for devotion and prayer will strengthen the bonds of a family beyond what you can imagine. One night recently, my wife and I were in our bedroom having our nightly devotion. Four of our children (the ones still at home), all teenagers, were sitting on our bed listening and asking questions about the Lord and about the Bible. When they left the room, Lisa turned to me and said, "Do you realize that all of our teenage children are in our room on a Friday night talking about the Lord?"

At that moment, the truth of that old saying became as real to me as any other. Only God could make this happen. I remember when I was their age. Most Friday nights I was not even at home, much less interested in talking to my parents about the Lord. Don't misunderstand me. My teenagers are not perfect by any means, and we struggle with life's challenges just like all families. The difference is that they have allowed God to guide them in spite of their parent's failures.

The Christian's Responsibility to the Church

In Hebrews 10:25 the Bible gives us a clear commandment about gathering together with other believers: "Not forsaking the assembling of ourselves together, as the manner of some is; but exhorting one another: and so much the more, as ye see the day approaching." We have a responsibility to meet with other believers to worship God together as one body. Just as there is strength in numbers in the armed forces, so there is strength in numbers in our churches and among believers. Jesus promised, "For where two or three are gathered together in my name, there am I in the midst of them" (Matthew 13:40).

Now although I do not have it all figured out, there is a theme throughout the Bible regarding "pairs" (groups of two). It began way back in Genesis in the Garden of Eden when the Lord said that it was not good for man to be alone and thus created Eve for Adam. And so it is for us Christians: It is not good that we are alone. We need fellowship with other believers to gain strength and encourage one another. What's more, Jesus promised in Matthew 13:40 that

He would be among us when we gather. I don't know about you, but I wait eagerly for Sunday and Wednesday so that I can gather together with those of like faith and worship our Lord and Savior Jesus Christ. Remember that we are to be a *unit* working together for Christ. When I am weak, they lift me up. When I am fallen, they carry me. Our church is a well of water that refreshes us and the table where our souls are nourished. God has ordained it so.

4

TRAINING TIPS

We must prepare ourselves for the battle. We must be ready in season and out of season. 2 Timothy 4:2 tells us: "Preach the word; be instant in season, out of season; reprove, rebuke, exhort with all longsuffering and doctrine." Why? Because the devil is waiting for an opportunity to devour you and make you useless for the Lord. 1 Peter 5:8 says, "Be sober, be vigilant; because your adversary the devil, as a roaring lion, walketh about, seeking whom he may devour." So how do we prepare and train for battle? In three ways: We must watch and pray daily; we must read *and* study the Bible (there is a difference); and we must worship our Lord in spirit and in truth.

Watch And Pray

A soldier's life is simple, really. While we were in garrison I did not have to give a moment's thought wondering what the day would hold for me. At 6:00 AM sharp each morning we had formation for physical training. Physical training lasted an hour, and then we were released for breakfast ("chow," as we called it). At 8:30 AM we had formation again at our place of work. A Christian soldier should have a routine that mirrors that of a military soldier. Rather than physical training we should spend an hour a day in the morning or evening exercising our spirit (Matthew 26:41). Spiritual exercise will prepare our heart and mind for the day ahead. It is much like physical training in that, although we exert a lot of energy doing the exercise, our body actually gains energy so that we are less tired throughout the day. Spiritual exercise refreshes the heart and renews the mind. It prepares us for what life has for us that particular day and enables us to STAND when the temptations and trials come.

Read and Study

Reading and studying are actually two separate events. Reading is simply that – reading. Our daily Bible reading should be a few chapters a day. Though reading the Bible through in a year is admirable it is not required. Most often my Bible reading leads me to several topics to study on. I enjoy studying a topic thoroughly from start to finish. Reading and studying *should* be two separate events. Your study time should not replace your reading time and vice versa. Here is why. When we pray, we speak to God. When we read our Bibles, God speaks to us. First, God's word gives us direction. Psalm 119:105 says, "Thy word is a lamp unto my feet, and a light unto my path." Through His word God reveals to us what He would have us do each day. Secondly, most of us spend more time asking God to do something than we do thanking Him for what He has already done. So the amount of time you should spending reading will depends on how many things you have asked God to do. Why? Because God will respond to your prayer requests through His word. That is how you get the answers you seek. This is not to say that if we never ask God for anything we shouldn't read our Bibles.

Studying is a result of reading. You will select a topic from your reading or something that God has spoken to your heart about to explore in depth. Studying could also arise from something you heard in church that leads you to want to discover everything the Bible has to say about the subject. I love studying the word of God – so much so that I have to stop and make sure I have also read my Bible that day. One does not replace the other. 2 Timothy 2:15 says, "Study to shew thyself approved unto God, a workman that needeth not to be ashamed, rightly dividing the word of truth."

Why do we study? We study so that we can give an answer – based on the truth of God's word – to someone who asks us a question. 1 Peter 3:15

says, "But sanctify the Lord God in your hearts: and be ready always to give an answer to every man that asketh you a reason of the hope that is in you with meekness and fear." Recall that the "purpose" of this book is to provide you with a basic training in the truth of the "the sword of the Spirit, which is the word of God" (in Ephesians 6:17). That is our primary offensive weapon. A soldier is useless without his weapons. We have other weapons in our arsenal that you might want to study for yourself. Psalm 127:5 mentions one such weapon.

Worship in Spirit and in Truth

Jesus tells us that "God is a Spirit: and they that worship him must worship him in spirit and in truth" (John 4:24). So what exactly does that mean? How do we worship God in spirit? I would venture to say that we worship him with every part of our being. Many Christians "play church" and put on a good front. Many who are diligent about attendance, tithing, and working around the church neglect the moving of the Holy Spirit. The truth is that God does not care as much about those former things as He does about our personal relationship with Him. You see, God does not see as we see. God looks on what is on the inside of a person, not what is on the outside. 1 Samuel 16:7 says, "But the LORD said unto Samuel, Look not on his countenance, or on the height of his stature; because I have refused him: for the LORD seeth not as man seeth; for man looketh on the outward appearance, but the LORD looketh on the heart." So to be fully prepared for battle, we must have our heart in the right place. Our spirit must be focused on the Lord. We must not neglect the moving of the Holy Spirit. When we are prompted to do something for the Lord, we must not ignore His nudge. If we do so, we will soon grieve the Holy Spirit and become numb to His calling.

The "truth" Jesus spoke of in John 4:24 is not a reference to the word of God but refers rather to being honest with ourselves and with those around us. We must be honest with the Lord about our condition. We must confess our sins to Him and come clean with all of our transgressions. If we dare to get honest with one another, we will all admit that we fall often and sin against the Lord. I cling to this verse when I have not done what I know I should have done or have done something that I know I should not have done. 1 John 2:1 says, "My little children, these things write I unto you, that ye sin not. And if any man sin, we have an advocate with the Father, Jesus Christ the righteous." Praise God! Praise God! Praise God! How longsuffering is our Lord! How merciful, how loving, how truly wonderful it is to be born again through the precious blood of the Lamb! He is righteous! He is worthy! Just be honest with Him and He will forgive you so that you can worship Him the way He desires and deserves.

5

IDENTIFY THE ENEMY

Ironically, the first task listed in the *Soldier's Manual of Common Tasks* is "See." See refers to being able to identify and report enemy activity. In the military, acronyms are golden and so, of course, we had one for this task: S-A-L-U-T-E. S-A-L-U-T-E stands for Size, Activity, Location, Unit, Time, and Equipment. Although it is nearly impossible to draw a parallel between S-A-L-U-T-E and the Christian soldier, what would a soldier's manual be without a few acronyms, right? We'll see if we can't come up with some later. For now, let's focus on the topic – identifying your enemy.

My son-in-law is a United States Marine. He has served in Fallujah in the Iraq War and has told me that one of the most difficult issues our troops face is identifying the enemy – distinguishing him from the average citizens. That is an important truth in spiritual warfare as well.

Everything we experience in the world today is a reflection of our spiritual condition. I would venture to say that is a reflection of the spiritual condition of the church. The way we categorize sin is very different today from how we did it even just 20 years ago. Isaiah 5:20 says, "Woe unto them that call evil good, and good evil; that put darkness for light, and light for darkness; that put bitter for sweet, and sweet for bitter! "Every Christian soldier should be able to identify the enemy when he is near. They ought to know his characteristics and how he presents himself. Every military soldier knows how to identify enemy troops. In fact, we studied so intensely that we could identify them from a great way off. So let's define our enemy here so that we know what to look for and how to identify him. Let's begin our "reconnaissance mission" in the book of Genesis, chapter 3.

Genesis 3:1 says, "Now the serpent was more subtil than any beast of the field which the LORD God had made. And he said unto the woman, Yea, hath God said, Ye shall not eat of every tree of the garden?"

He's Subtle and Crafty

What can we draw from this one passage of scripture? First, the enemy is *subtle*. By definition subtle means "cunning, wily, or crafty." That is very good starting point for identifying the enemy. We now know that he is far too crafty to simply come right out and say, "I am the devil and am here to tempt you to sin and wreak havoc on your life." He will disguise himself as something that is *supposed* to be there. In Eden He concealed himself as a serpent. No doubt Adam and Eve had been around such serpents and so it was nothing strange to see them wandering about.

Likewise, the devil will use what is around you to tempt you into sin. One of the devil's slyest tricks is to get you to do the right thing at the wrong time. Here's an example, the Bible says that we are to pray and study. The Bible also says that we are to obey those in authority over us (Ephesians 6:5). So is it right for you to pray and read your Bible while you are on the clock at work? Everything has its time and place. Your testimony for the Lord will be much stronger if your fellow workers see you working diligently while on the clock and reading your Bible and praying during breaks and lunchtime. The devil would like nothing more than to see you ruin your testimony with your co-workers by giving them reason to find fault with your work ethic. God knows and in fact has ordained that we must work to live (Genesis 3:19).

He Casts Doubt

Second, the enemy *casts doubt* (the opposite of faith). Notice that the serpent asked Eve a question. He asked it in such a way as to cast doubt on the words of God. The devil will always cast doubt on what God tells you to do. Note how the devil conveniently omitted the rest of what God commanded Adam not to do. Let's look at the passage again. "Now the serpent was more subtil than any beast of the field which the LORD God had made. And he said unto the woman, Yea, **hath God said**, Ye shall not eat of every tree of the garden?" (Genesis 3:1).

Now let's compare that with what God *actually* said in Genesis 2:15-17 (emphasis added):

> "And the LORD God took the man, and put him into the garden of Eden to dress it and to keep it. And the LORD God commanded the man, saying, *Of every tree of the garden thou mayest freely eat: But of the tree of the knowledge of good and evil, thou shalt not eat of it: for in the day that thou eatest thereof thou shalt surely die.*"

The Lord did in fact say that they could eat of every tree of the garden, but the devil left out the rest of what God said. Now let's look at Eve's response to the serpent (Genesis 3:2-5):

> "And the woman said unto the serpent, We may eat of the fruit of the trees of the garden: But of the fruit of the tree which is in the midst of the garden, God hath said, Ye shall not eat of it, neither shall ye touch it, lest ye die. And the serpent said unto the woman, Ye shall not surely die: For God doth know that in the day ye eat thereof, then your eyes shall be opened, and ye shall be as gods, knowing good and evil."

Close, Eve, but not quite! Look what Eve does in verse 3: she *adds* to the words of God. Now it is not clear whether Adam in his zeal had told Eve not to touch it or Eve just decided to add those words herself under the influence of the serpent. When he heard that Eve added to what God said the devil knew immediately that she was susceptible to his tricks. So he exploited her gullibility and cast his own spin on what God said: "ye shall not surely die: For God doth know that in the day ye eat thereof, then your eyes shall be opened, and ye shall be as gods, knowing good and evil."

So before moving onto the next characteristic of the enemy, let's recap. He is cunning, sly, and deceitful. He disguises himself as something familiar to us. He puts doubt in our mind about what God has told us to do. And he adds to and omits from the words of God to accomplish his own goal.

My wife and I had the privilege recently of escorting our church's youth group on a mission trip to Nashville, TN. We settled on Nashville because our pastor's wife told us about a wonderful ministry there that feeds the homeless under a specific bridge and holds a worship service every Tuesday. What a wonderful way to minister to the lost! We thought this would be a great way to help our teens realize that they ought to appreciate what God has given them.

I was somewhat apprehensive because we had only been attending the church for a short time and since I had just begun working with the youth I really did not know what to expect. As you probably know, teenagers are very unpredictable. During the trip, one young lady became so burdened for the homeless people we were serving that she surrendered to God's work. A few weeks after we returned home from the trip, during our Wednesday night youth group meeting, I could tell something was wrong with her. We finished the lesson and after the altar call she asked to speak with me about something that was troubling her. She began talking with my wife so I waited a few minutes before I was led to join the conversation. Just a few weeks after surrendering to God's work this young lady was struggling with doubts about her own salvation.

In my time ministering to others, I have learned that such situations are difficult to handle. We who work in any form of Christian ministry do not want to talk anybody out of their salvation or lead them to believe they are saved when they are not. After hearing this young lady's testimony, however, it was evident that she was saved and that the devil had been putting doubts in her head about her eternal security. How many saints of God have fallen to this same temptation? While I do not presume to speak for every Christian, I know that many of us have been assaulted with the same doubts shortly after being saved. One of the oldest weapons the devil has in his arsenal is to make you doubt the promises of God regarding your salvation. Romans 8:33-39 makes this promise of God clear. The Apostle Paul says that neither height, nor depth, nor any other creature, shall be able to separate us from the love of God. This truth is confirmed in Ephesians 4:30 in which the Lord tells us that we are sealed by the Holy Spirit of God unto the day of redemption.

The very next week, God laid a special message on my heart for the youth group regarding eternal security of those who have trusted the Lord for salvation. In order to prove the point, I had them turn in their Bibles to Genesis chapter 1. We read verse 3: "And God said, let there be light: and there was light." Then in verse 11: "God said, let the earth bring forth grass, the herb yielding seed, and the fruit tree yielding fruit after his kind, whose seed is in itself, upon the earth: and it was so." I then asked the youth this question: "Do you believe that the sun will rise tomorrow." They all confirmed that they believed it would. "Why?" I asked. They responded, "Because God said it would." Just then I knew that the message was sinking in. We then turned in our Bibles to Romans 10:13: "For whosoever shall call upon the name of the Lord shall be saved." I asked them to tell me the difference between what God said in Genesis 1:3 and what He said in Romans 10:13? The light came on in their eyes. I glanced over at the young lady who had doubted her salvation and saw a smile as wide as the Grand Canyon filling her face. The truth of God's word had pierced her heart and cast out any doubt she was having about her salvation. The truth of God's Word is sure and God cannot lie.

He Attacks When we are Most Vulnerable

Third, take special notice that the devil approached Eve when she was alone. He chose a time when Adam and Eve were not together to approach and "beguiled" Eve, not Adam. The enemy attacks when we are separated from those who hold us accountable. He attacks those closest to us in an effort to turn us away from God. For now, we will focus on how important it is for us to be with those who are of like mind and like faith. As mentioned earlier, Hebrews 10:25 says, "Not forsaking the assembling of ourselves together...." Be careful when you are alone, for this is when you are most venerable to the enemy's attack. Be careful of those who are closest to you. Hold each other accountable for your actions, attitudes, and worship of God. We draw strength from one another.

Jesus chose 12 men as close followers. In our quest to determine the deep meaning of the number of disciples and all our pondering about what the number 12 represents, we often overlook the simplest, most prominent reason that our Lord selected 12. What is it? It is because the Lord knows that we are stronger when we have others of like faith around us with whom we can spend time and worship the Lord. How's *that* for deep?

During basic training, each of us was assigned a "battle buddy." Like a shadow, battle buddies went everywhere and did everything together. This was the case only during basic training, not when we completed training. During training it was good to have someone on whom we could rely and depend. The devil would like nothing more than for you to be out of fellowship with other Christians and with God. If he can get you to stay out of church for one Sunday worship service or one mid-week Bible study or prayer meeting, rest assured that he will. And I can guarantee if you've been saved for any length of time, you likely face more temptation on the day before or the day of a church event or service.

Let's get one thing clear: THE DEVIL HATES YOU AND WANTS TO DESTROY YOU!!! He waited until Adam and Eve were separated from one another and then preyed on the weaker of the two (and, for the record, this is not always and necessarily the woman). Though the timing of the fatal encounter recorded in Genesis 3 is not clear, I am sure the devil did not approach Eve with his cunning proposition all of sudden. I am sure he worked on Eve slowly, over the course of days, weeks, or months, creeping in unawares and warming up to her.... And then, when the timing was just right: BAM! HE STRIKES!

The devil has not changed his ways. In fact, he has been working the same trickery he used on Adam and Eve to deceive Christians throughout the ages.

He Makes Himself Seem Bigger than He is

The enemy presents himself as bigger than he is. 1 Peter 5:8 says, "Be sober, be vigilant; because your adversary the devil, as a roaring lion, walketh about, seeking whom he may devour." Though we should never take our enemy lightly, we must always remember the truth that "because greater is he that is in you, than he that is in the world" (1 John 4:4). The Bible assures us that we will never be tempted beyond what we are able to stand and that God will always make a way of escape. 1 Corinthians 10:13 says, "There hath no temptation taken you but such as is common to man: but God is faithful, who will not suffer you to be tempted above that ye are able; but will with the temptation also make a way to escape, that ye may be able to bear it." (For a great exposition of this truth, I highly recommend Evangelist Paul Schwanke's book *As a Roaring Lion*).

As I mentioned earlier, the devil will often try to get you to do the right thing at the wrong time. A perfect example of this tactic is in Matthew 4:1-11 that records the devil's temptation of Jesus. I will not quote the entire passage but want you to pay special attention to the three temptations our Lord faced, each of which, in its own time and right place, would not have been sin. Because of the timing, however, if Jesus had yielded to the temptations He would have sinned. It was nothing for Jesus to change stones into bread. He did something similar later in the gospels when he fed the 5,000 (and if He could bring Lazarus who had been dead for days back to life, turning stones to bread would have not been so difficult). And Jesus could certainly have dived off the top of the temple only to be swooped up by a host of angels. That wouldn't have been a sin … in the right time. Lastly, it was certainly not sin for Jesus to take dominion over all the kingdoms of the world. After all, they are His to take…. But *not yet*. Read through the passage for a better understanding. Yielding to these temptations at the time of the devil's choosing, however, would have interfered with the mission that He had left heaven to accomplish.

He is a Liar: The Father of Lies

Lastly, I want to point out that the devil is a liar. John 8:44 states, "Ye are of your father the devil, and the lusts of your father ye will do. He was a murderer from the beginning, and abode not in the truth, because there is no truth in him. When he speaketh a lie, he speaketh of his own: for he is a liar, and the father of it." As we saw in the beginning of this chapter, Satan turns, twists, omits, and adds to the words of God to accomplish his own purpose. Don't think for a moment that the devil does not know the word of God. He knows it better than all learned Bible scholars in the world and certainly knows it better than you and I. 2 Corinthians 11:14 says, "And no marvel; for Satan himself is transformed into an angel of light."

The Enemy's Characteristics in Review

- Practices deception with sly and cunning tactics

- Uses something familiar to you to tempt you

- Casts doubt on God's Word

- Makes us doubt our salvation

- Omits and adds to God's Word

- Attacks when we are alone

- Attacks those closest to you

- Lies and distorts the truth

- Appears as an angel of light

- Distracts the saints of God and keeps them preoccupied with "Lesser" things

6

COMMUNICATE

As soldiers in the US Army, we were taught a specific way to communicate and steeped in communication discipline. We learned what is known as the phonetic alphabet. Most people recognize a few letters of the phonetic alphabet (for example, from police shows where the officer pursuing a fleeing suspect gives the dispatcher the license plate number in phonetics) such as A=Alpha, B=Bravo, C=Charlie, D=Delta, and E=Echo. The letters have corresponding words for purposes of clarity. The battlefield is often noisy and messages are easily misunderstood. A simple communication error can have deadly results for a unit if supporting fire is called to the wrong location.

During my duty in Operation Desert Storm I witnessed such a tragedy. We had stopped to assist and repair a tank that had lost power. After we completed the repairs, which took nearly six hours, we attempted to reunite with our unit from the rear. We caught up with them just as they and several Apache helicopters were engaging enemy forces on a ridge somewhere in southern Iraq. For those not familiar with the Army and wartime communication, armored vehicles or ground troops fire a green flare to signal that they are "friendly" forces. As we crested the ridge, we quickly realized that we were much too close to the front lines and were in no position to defend ourselves from enemy fire.

As we reversed course and made our way to the rear of our tank line, I had the opportunity to watch the battle from a unique vantage point. What I witnessed I will never forget. As we traveled along the ridge, our Apache helicopters were firing on enemy troops. At some point during the battle the formation was broken, and one of our tanks got out of position. I witnessed an Apache fire on our tank. Just as the missile was deployed, I saw our tank fire off a green star cluster to signal it was friendly. Unfortunately, it was too late. The tank was struck by a missile from its own comrades. I do not know the outcome of the troops aboard the tank. Reports estimate that 24% of the casualties sustained by US troops in Operation Desert Storm result from friendly fire. Considering there were only 148 casualties overall, 24% is a tragically high number. It is likely that most such incidents resulted from poor communication and not correctly identifying the enemy.

How many friendly fire casualties has the church suffered over the years? I would venture to say much more than 24%. Clear, godly communication is critical in a Christian soldier's life – not only for one's own survival but for the survival of those fighting alongside us on the battlefield.

Communication with our Commander

The most important element of communication is our ability to communicate clearly our position on the battlefield with our Commander. In Chapter 3, in the section Watch and Pray, we discussed communicating our position with God. We must know where we stand at all times. God forbid that we would think we are standing when in fact we have fallen. I am referring to our heart being right with God *before* we enter the battlefield. Communication with our Commander must be a two-way conversation. I recently told our youth group that praying is our way of speaking with God our Father whereas reading our Bible is His way of speaking with us. Most of us participate in only one-way communication with God. We speak to God and do not allow Him to speak with us. And we wonder why we don't hear from Him.

Let's discuss for a moment our special way of communicating with our Commander. Jesus Himself gave us a template if you will for our communication with our Father in heaven in Matthew 6:9-13: "After this manner therefore pray ye: Our Father which art in heaven, Hallowed be thy name. Thy kingdom come. Thy will be done in earth, as it is in heaven. Give us this day our daily bread. And forgive us our debts, as we forgive our debtors. And lead us not into temptation, but deliver us from evil: for thine is the kingdom, and the power, and the glory, for ever. Amen."

Much of what we pray never penetrates the roof of the building we're in. Why? Because we pray selfishly with more concern about our own agenda than the will of God being fulfilled in our lives. James 4:3 reveals this truth to us: "Ye ask, and receive not, because ye ask amiss, that ye may consume it upon your lusts."

To avoid asking "amiss," let's follow the template Jesus provided us:

"Our Father which art in heaven, Hallowed by thy name."

Every prayer should start with an expression of our reverence for God the Father. We should thank Him for His goodness, mercy, and longsuffering for us. We should thank Him for our salvation and that of our family. We should thank Him because He is worthy to be praised!!! Try it and you will find that your prayer time will be much more fulfilling than it is today.

"Thy kingdom come. Thy will be done in earth, as it is in heaven."

We should always seek the Lord's will for our lives. Pray for God to reveal *His* will for your life. The sooner we begin seeking God's will for our life, the better. Sadly, most Christians live in God's *permissive* will rather than in God's *perfect* will. I strongly believe that God has a perfect will for every person's life. At a certain point and time, God gives us the opportunity to choose His perfect will. What we do with that choice is completely up to us. Many things will happen during this time in our life. We will have many other choices – besides God's perfect will – will be available to us and the devil will present many alternatives and many temptations aimed to lead us astray. How we respond and the decision we make will send us down the road that we will travel the rest of our life.

"Give us this day our daily bread."

Notices that there was no mention of a new car, new boat, new shoes, or new house. Jesus advised us to take no thought for what we shall eat, drink, or wear (Matthew 6:26-34). He will provide for us the essentials of life. He promised to do so.

"And forgive us our debts, as we forgive our debtors"

God forgives us only on account of His mercy and grace. We are *all* unworthy. This line always reminds me of another scripture, Luke 6:37, which says, "Judge not, and ye shall not be judged: condemn not, and ye shall not be condemned: forgive, and ye shall be forgiven." Likewise, in Matthew 7:1-5 Jesus tells us that we need to look at our own faults before we point out others' faults. How critical we can be of others at times. Brother, this ought not to be so. If we expect the Lord to hear our prayers, we need to cleanse our hearts of all such judgments.

"And lead us not into temptation, but deliver us from evil"

I pray each day that the Lord would build a hedge around my family and those that I love so they would not be tempted of the devil. Now of course I know that the Lord will allow them to be tried and tested, but my prayer is for their safety and security and that they might stand and be bold in that hour.

"for thine is the kingdom, and the power, and the glory, for ever. Amen."

Our prayers should end just as they started – praising God for His mercy, His longsuffering, His grace, and His power to last the day without falling on the field of battle.

Communication Discipline

We must learn communication discipline. We considered *how* we should pray. Now let's turn our attention to *when* we should pray. The answer, found in 1 Thessalonians 5:17, is simple: "Pray without ceasing." Romans 12:12 says, "Rejoicing in hope; patient in tribulation; continuing instant in prayer." A soldier must be in constant communication with "headquarters," if you will. Our Commander in Chief (God) has the ultimate "open door" policy. If we open the door, He will sup with us and let us sup with Him (Revelation 3:20). We can learn a lesson on when to pray from one of the greatest soldiers in the Bible, King David. In Psalms 55:17 David gives us some guidance as to when to pray: "Evening, and morning, and at noon, will I pray, and cry aloud: and he shall hear my voice."

Personally I find it easiest and most fulfilling to pray early in the morning when there are no distractions and plenty of time to spend time with the Lord. You find the time that works best for you ... and *pray without ceasing!*

Communicating with Others

Lastly, I often marvel at the way family members speak to one another. We often communicate more politely and with more respect to strangers than to members of our own family. As Christians, our testimony is probably more important within our family than it is within our social relationships (friends and fellow church members) and our work relationships (boss, coworkers, and employees). If we were saved later in life, our family members often know all the "issues" we had in the past and are quick to "remind" us how we used to be. We need to make sure that we communicate appropriately with our family so as not offend them and turn them away from the Lord. Your family will be the most difficult to turn to the Lord. Colossians 4:6 says, "Let your speech *be* alway with grace, seasoned with salt, that ye may know how ye ought to answer every man." Let's start communicating grace-fully with our own family members!

7

NAVIGATE

Our unit had been in the middle of the Saudi desert for about three weeks with little to no information about what was going on when my sergeant and I received orders from our commander to go refill our water trailer because we were running low. The orders came in sometime around 1 or 2 PM and we began making preparations to go. We left our encampment around 3 PM and wanted to get back before sunset. Just before leaving, we scoped out the vast sand dunes, and then my sergeant motioned toward a location in the distance and told me to head in that direction. The desert in Saudi Arabia, unlike that in Arizona and California, is very deceiving. Although the terrain looks flat, it is actually a succession of very large rolling dunes. So, at the time, my sergeant's directions seemed a bit vague. There was nothing but sand as far as the eye could see in every direction.

We traveled for about 45 minutes and then paused. Looking back towards our camp, we could see nothing. Looking forward to where we were supposed to be going, nothing. We were lost. My sergeant looked me in the eye and confessed that he was not sure we were going the right way. "Wonderful!" I thought, but didn't dare utter it out loud. At that time, soldiers didn't speak their mind or backtalk superiors. (A lot has changed since then, I hear.) Nevertheless, he finally pulled out the map that marked the location of the camp with the water replenishing tanks. I learned later that before we left, the commander had given my sergeant specific grid coordinates to lead from our camp to the water camp. In order for the grid coordinates to work, however, you must first know where you are or have a landmark from which to plot a route. So we had to follow our tracks back to our camp and then start over again. This provides a great illustration of why we must make sure that we follow our map and the instructions that our Commander has given us.

Every soldier must learn basic land navigation. In order to navigate unfamiliar terrain, a soldier must use two tools the military provides — a map and a compass. With a basic understanding of how to use these tools a soldier will never be lost in the wilderness. Like military soldiers, we Christian soldiers are provided with the necessary tools to navigate our way through the battlefield. In this case our tools are the Bible and the Holy Spirit. The Bible is our map; the Holy Spirit, the compass. The Bible shows the hills and the valleys, and the Holy Spirit provides the route we should take.

Would to God that every Christian — myself included — could remain on the mountaintop and never have to go through hills, valleys, and desert places. But our Lord would not have it so because He knows that we would gain no ground. Down in the valley is where the soldier's strength is increased and his training is exercised. We will find more water (which is a type of the Holy Spirit, Ephesians 5:26) in the valley than on the mountaintop.

A topographical map is the most common type of map used in the US military. The topographical map represents the lay of the land using a series of lines to depict the elevation changes on the earth. To read this type of map, a soldier must first understand its features. Topographical maps have standard terrain features, including, spurs, cliffs, ridges, hills, saddles, valleys, depressions, and draws. The two most obvious terrain features are hills and valleys. The ability to understand the lines on a topographical map enables a soldier to stay out of harm's way as he navigates his way to the chosen destination.

Similarly, Christian soldiers must understand the basic features of the Bible in order to find their way. The two features that have helped me understand the Bible more than any other are: (1) *dispensational truth* (2 Timothy 2:15) and (2) *understanding that all scriptures have three applications* (2 Timothy 3:16). A dispensation can be defined as the way God deals with His people during a certain period of time. There are two key dispensations in human history – the dispensation of Law and the dispensation of Grace. Throughout most of the Old Testament the children of Israel were under the law. God gave the law to Moses to give to the Children of Israel (Exodus 19). When Jesus Christ died on the cross God's way of dealing with His children changed. Please under-stand that the law was a schoolmaster intended to lead them to Christ and was never meant to be the way of salvation for God's people. Galatians 3:24 states: "Wherefore the law was our schoolmaster *to bring us* unto Christ, that we might be justified by faith." Salvation has always been by grace through faith (Galatians 3:25). For a better understanding of the faith of the Old Testament saints, see Hebrews 11.

At Christ's death, God established a new covenant with the world. God no longer requires you to keep the law – which you could not do anyway – but rather to repent of your sins and believe on His Son the Lord Jesus Christ for salvation (Hebrews 1:1-2; 9:16).

A dispensational understanding of the scriptures will help us realize that even though all scripture is profitable for instruction, reproof, rebuke, and exhortation and can teach us how to live it is not all directed at us. In addition, it helps to understand that every passage in the Bible has three applications: Historical, Doctrinal, and Spiritual. Understanding these two features will enable us to read the map with a clear perspective and avoid dangerous terrain on the battlefield (2 Timothy 4:3).

The Holy Bible (our map)

The Bible instructs us to study to show ourselves approved unto God so that we will not be ashamed and rightly divide the word of God (2 Timothy 2:15). This verse has several implications. First, it tells us that *we must study the word*. As noted in Chapter 4: Training Tips, there is a difference between reading and studying. Studying implies that we are to find the root of the mat-ter and diligently search out the answers to our questions. Think about that concept for just a moment. When we study a subject or topic in the Bible, what is it that we are really looking for? We study to find the deeper meaning –the truth, God's truth – about the topic as revealed in a passage of scripture. Without fail, each and every time I study a topic, I find the Lord Jesus Christ and how to apply the truth to my life. He is the root of the matter. John 5:39 says, "Search the scriptures; for in them ye think ye have eternal life: and they are they which testify of me."

When I began to think about the root, I stepped outside my front door and stared at some of the plants in my flower beds. I noticed that for the most part roots cannot be seen because they are underground. Without the roots, however, what was visible above ground – the plant, the tree, the flower – would not be alive. If I watered only the leaves of the plant, the plant would not last long. And so it is with our lives. We Christian soldiers need to water our roots. We must study the Bible and be well grounded in sound doctrine. (Ephesians 3:17)(Colossians 2:6,7).

We must water those roots often. Jeremiah 17:8 says, "For he shall be as a tree planted by the waters, and that spreadeth out her roots by the river, and shall not see when heat cometh, but her leaf shall be green; and shall not be careful in the year of drought, **neither shall cease from yielding fruit**."

Sometimes only that which is growing beneath what we can see on the surface is good for food. Sometimes the root is the food. The carrot and potato are much more delicious and nutritious than the greenery we see above the surface. When you search out a matter with a pure heart and clean motives, God finds great delight in revealing His truth to you. I am amazed at the truth God has revealed to me when I study in this manner. God reveals the answers to all of life's problems in the scriptures, but we must find them and ask for His guidance. Here is where the Holy Spirit comes into the picture (John 16:13). Without the guidance of the Holy Spirit, our efforts will be in vain.

In addition to telling us that we should study the scriptures, 2 Timothy 2:15, tells us that *we should rightly divide the scriptures*. In his book *Rightly*

Dividing, Clarence Larkin provides an excellent description of what it means to "rightly divide" the word of God. I highly recommend this book to you and encourage you to pray as you read it and learn how to rightly divide the Bible. Understanding that there are clear divisions in the scriptures will help you navigate the Bible and put God's word in perspective. For example, many Christians are most confused by the four gospels —Matthew, Mark, Luke, and John. Within these gospels Jesus used many parables to get His message across to the nation of Israel. Many misapplications of Jesus' teachings have confused Christians and led them down the wrong path. Even without a deep knowledge of the various divisions in the Bible, a Christian can simply find the answer to the alleged "contradictions" in the gospels by applying the truth found in Hebrew 9:14-18. (Emphasis added)

> "How much more shall the blood of Christ, who through the eternal Spirit offered himself without spot to God, purge your conscience from dead works to serve the living God? And for this cause he is the mediator of the new testament, that by means of death, for the redemption of the transgressions that were under the first testament, they which are called might receive the promise of eternal inheritance. For where a testament is, there must also of necessity be the death of the testator. *For a testament is of force after men are dead: otherwise it is of no strength at all while the testator liveth.* Whereupon neither the first testament was dedicated without blood."

To sum up the passage on rightly dividing and considering the Bible from a dispensational perspective: Everything recorded in the gospels before Christ's death, burial, and resurrection falls under the Old Testament law. The birth of our Lord did not establish the New Testament but rather marked the beginning of God's offering of His dear Son, the Lord Jesus Christ. As stated in Hebrews 9:16-17, the New Testament was not in force until Christ died and rose again. Only *after* His resurrection did God offer salvation by grace through faith (Ephesians 2:8). It was God's grace to give us His Son, and by faith we believe on Him.

To show that the events in the four gospels apply to the dispensation of Law, let's turn to Matthew 19:16-17. A man came to Jesus and asked how he may have eternal life. Notice Jesus' answer: "Keep the commandments." During Christ's life, to be right with God a man had to keep the Old Testament law. The sacrifice for our sins had not yet been offered, the blood of Jesus Christ had not yet been presented to the Father, and the work that Christ came to do (fulfill the law) had not yet been accomplished. This is not to say that we should not live according to the law, but rather that we are no longer kept safe by keeping the law and are now justified, sanctified, and redeemed by God's grace through faith – repenting of our sins and believing on the One who fulfilled the law.

Every map, both civilian and military, has a legend with certain symbols that represent a meaning. The symbols are used in lieu of words so that readers of the map can get a grasp of what is in that particular area. For example, a soldier always needs to identify sources of water on a map so that they can replenish their water supply. An army cannot move without water. For the most part, water is supplied by support troops from the rear. When the battle is raging or when supply lines have been cut off, however, a soldier must find natural sources of water. The symbol for water, like all others, is universal so that you will be able to locate it no matter which military map you are looking at. This truth is evident in the scriptures. No matter what is going on in our lives, no matter which book of the Bible we are reading, one thing remains consistent throughout: *Christ remains the same.* What changes is not Christ but the terrain in which we find ourselves.

We must also have a basic understanding of how to apply scriptures from both the Old Testament and the gospels to our life. 2 Timothy 3:16 says, "All scripture is given by inspiration of God, and is profitable for doctrine, for reproof, for correction, for instruction in righteousness." Every verse or passage of scripture has three applications: Doctrinal, Spiritual, and Historical. Doctrinally, we must know to whom God was talking and what dispensation they were under. Misapplication of scripture has given rise to many false religions and cults and will only confuse a soldier of Christ. More times than not, in the Old Testament and the gospels, God is speaking to the children of

Israel regarding their salvation as a nation. Many Christians today forget that the nation of Israel is still God's chosen people. While God has set them aside for a time (Romans 11:25) as He deals with the Gentiles, once the "fullness of the Gentile be come in" God will once again turn to the nation of Israel. That being said, I can still apply those scriptures to myself and my life spiritually as a soldier of Christ.

The Holy Spirit (our compass)

Let's turn again to the illustration I shared at the beginning of the chapter of how my sergeant and I got lost in the desert on our water mission. I didn't mention that when we found ourselves lost my sergeant pulled out his compass, that other basic tool for land navigation. From our lost position, he tried to use the compass to navigate to the water point. That was futile. Why? Because to use the compass properly requires that you first know where you are. Now the compass is a great tool, but it is best used in conjunction with a map. The two are really inseparable. The Bible says in John 16:13, "Howbeit when he, the Spirit of truth, is come, he will guide you into all truth: for he shall not speak of himself; but whatsoever he shall hear, that shall he speak: and he will shew you things to come." And in John 14:6 Jesus said, "I am the way, the truth, and the life: no man cometh unto the Father, but by me."

From these two verses of scripture we see that the word and the Holy Spirit work together to guide us –to eternal life through our Lord and Savior Jesus Christ and to our heavenly Father. So how does the Holy Spirit accomplish this? The Holy Spirit guides us into the truth. Jesus said in John 17:17, "Sanctify them through thy truth: thy word is truth." So we see that the Holy Spirit testifies of the Lord Jesus Christ who in turn shows us the way because He is the way, the truth, and the life. You cannot have one without the other. There is absolutely no way that you can find your way or navigate through this world successfully without the Holy Spirit (your Compass) to point you in the right direction and you cannot find out where you are at without a map (the Bible, God's word). Knowing this truth is indispensable to the soldier of Christ. We must allow the Holy Spirit to guide us across the battlefield. We must submit what we "think" to what the Bible tells us is right.

2 Timothy 2:15: "Study to shew thyself approved unto God, a workman that needeth not to be ashamed, rightly dividing the word of truth."

Historical = It really did happen and applies to a specific people or person.

Doctrinal = Rules or principles that form a basis of belief.

Spiritual = All scripture can be used to help my personal walk with the Lord.

Oh, yes, to finish the story: My sergeant and I eventually found the other encampment, refilled our water supply, and made it back to camp just before dark.

8

BATTLEFIELDS

A soldier must learn to fight on different battlefields. A major concern of the military when deploying troops to the deserts of Southwest Asia was whether the soldiers would be able to survive and win in the heat of the desert. When I was a mechanic on the M1A1 Abrams tank we had a disciplined preventive maintenance routine designed to keep the vehicles combat-ready. It was no different for the soldiers. Having a steady supply of water for the troops was the top concern for the US military. Though I had never personally trained in a desert environment, I knew (halfway) what to expect of the weather having lived the previous eight years in Arizona. The weather was not identical, but the change was not as dramatic for me as it was for soldiers from other parts of the country. Before being deployed to the desert, we completed several survival training classes to help us understand the environment so we would not be in shock when we arrived. I would love to be able to say that this preparedness training made the transition from Europe to Southwest Asia insignificant, but that was not the case. Though it made it easier there was still a drastic difference between the two environments. In addition, the soldiers' emotional state only exacerbated the situation. Most soldiers were not sure what to expect. Despite the fact that many of the troops put on a front as though they were eager to engage in battle the widespread restlessness and unease told a different story.

Likewise, we Christian soldiers must prepare for every situation and every circumstance and be ready to face the enemy in any environment. God knows this, which is why He allows things to happen in our lives that will prepare us for the conflict. As a younger man, I often wondered why God allowed certain things to happen in Christian people's lives. Many people, myself included, have faced financial and health difficulties. Why would God – the very One who loved us so much that He sent His own Son to die for us – allow such adverse situations to come into our lives? I struggled to come to terms with this dilemma until just a few years ago.

God allows various trials into our lives for several reasons. God is molding us, testing our faith, or using us as a testimony so that others will see His grace manifest in and through our lives. Even in times of peace when there is no threat of war, a soldier still trains for war. So it is with the Christian soldier. When we are not facing temptation from the devil, God allows trials in our lives that test our patience and try our faith. The Apostle Peter explained it this way: "That the trial of your faith, being much more precious than of gold that perisheth, though it be tried with fire, might be found unto praise and honour and glory at the appearing of Jesus Christ" (1 Peter 1:7). God wants you to be ready when the time comes for Him to use you.

How many battles would be won if the Army's soldiers retreated at every hint of conflict? God trains us for different situations so that when the time comes to take a stand for the Lord we will not retreat or fall. I could not truly comfort a person grieving the loss of a loved one until I had experienced such loss personally. I didn't know the deep sorrow of losing a parent until my own father passed. I didn't know how to comfort a parent with a wayward child until my children began rebelling against authority. I did not learn to trust God to supply all my needs until I had bare cupboards and no money to restock them. I didn't know how to be a friend to someone until I really needed a friend.

God allows these situations in our lives so that we may comfort each other and help one another. Most importantly, God allows these trials so that we will lean on Him and look to Him for help. Proverbs 3:5 says, "Trust in the LORD with all thine heart; and lean not unto thine own understanding." If you find yourself in the middle of a situation for which you have no answers, problems that you are unable to fix, or boxed in with seemingly no way out, look up and call upon the One who has the answers, the solutions, and is mighty enough to make a way out. If He can calm the sea, cause the sun to stand still, and raise the dead, He can certainly put food on your table.

Most of us must endure these "lessons" multiple times because we just aren't getting it, aren't learning what God is trying to teach us. For me personally, it's usually because I am stubborn, hard-headed, and want things to go *my* way. Instead of waiting on God to give us His answer – *the* answer – we devise our own plan and get into a mess that God has to fix when we finally realize that He was right all along. I have to sit back and chuckle when I look at my children and realize that every time they rebel, no matter how large or small, God is showing me how I am towards Him.

The battlefields that we face are not on some distant shore – they are here and now. There are two types of battlefields that we soldiers of Christ face: **inward** battlefields and **outward** battlefields. The outward battlefields are the mountains, valleys, and deserts that we find ourselves and our families in. The inward battlefields consist of courage, commitment, sanctification, separation, and sin. Let's take a few moment to examine each of these battlefields so that we will be able to identify where we are when we find ourselves in the heat of conflict.

Outward Battlefields

The Mountaintop

Any commanding officer in the military will tell you that the best position from which to gain control over an area is the mountaintop. Those who hold the mountaintop have control of the battlefield. When our troops occupy the mountaintop, the most important task – the top priority – is *holding* the mountaintop because to lose it is to lose control of the battle. When the enemy holds the mountaintop, on the other hand, the top priority is *capturing* the mountaintop. This military truth about maintaining and holding the mountaintop applies not just to military soldiers but to Christian soldiers as well. Let's explore how this operates.

We have all been on the mountaintop of victory in our lives. You know, those times when everything in our lives seems to be going great. We give God thanks for all He has done and for His great blessings on our lives. The sun is always shining at the summit above the clouds. There is no rain. All is well. Now the mountaintop is where we find the Glory of God. We read in Exodus 20-24 that Moses went up to Mount Sinai and the Glory of God covered the mountain. God revealed Himself to Moses (in part, of course) and it changed Moses from that day forward. The mountaintop is where the blessings of God are, wouldn't you agree? Don't we all want to live on the mountain with God? For the moment, save your decision on where we should dwell.

As we search the scriptures, we find another characteristic of dwelling on the mountaintop. In Genesis 22, we see Abraham going up to the mountaintop. He was going for a different reason. You see, the mountaintop is where some of the most difficult trials come. God had instructed Abraham to take his only son Isaac and place him on the altar to sacrifice to the Lord. Genesis 22:2 tells us that God said, "take now thy son, thine only son Isaac, whom thou lovest, and get thee into the land of Moriah; and offer him there for a burnt offering upon one of the mountains which I will tell thee of." If you have ever hiked to the top of the mountain, you know that when you get there, the wind blows hard in those higher elevations. Abraham experienced the wind of God blowing hard against him. Abraham's faith steadied him, however, and he obeyed God and the result was the same as it was for Moses. When he obeyed, Abraham saw the Glory of God, and God provided the sacrifice.

Let's turn to Matthew 4 in the New Testament and see something else that takes place on the mountaintop, something that every Christian must face: temptation. In Matthew 4:8-9, the Bible says, "Again, the devil taketh him up into an exceeding high mountain, and sheweth him all the kingdoms of the world, and the glory of them And saith unto him, All these things will I give thee, if thou wilt fall down and worship me." We know, of course, that Jesus resisted and gained the victory over the devil.

I have been warned many times to "be careful what you ask for." Each and every time I have been on the mountaintop, without fail, I was tempted with the pride of life (1 John 2:16). Something happens when we reach the top of that mountain. The devil whispers in our ear, "You did it." *You* did it. And if we are honest with ourselves most of us will admit that, if only for a moment, we did say, "I did it!" Then the Holy Spirit rebukes us and says, "*Who* did it?" Decision time. Will you take the glory or give *God* the glory? In our finite minds we see the mountaintop of victory as the most desirable place to dwell.

As we really study the scriptures, though, we find that this is the most dangerous battlefield of all. The longer we dwell on the mountain, the more we are tempted of the devil to take the glory for the victory that God has wrought in our lives. Because of this flesh that we still abide in, we are more susceptible to this temptation. Soldiers holding a defensive position slowly lose their ability to advance in battle and become complacent – content in a holding pattern. If you have ever been on the mountaintop, you know that food and water there are scarce. Your only source will be what you take with you. Again, be careful what you ask for.

The Valley

From the mountaintop, we have a great view of the valley and the plains of the desert below. Most of us consider the valley a less desirable place to be than the mountain. We have considered the mountaintops and the dangers present there. Yet those in the valley always want to get to the mountaintop. Interestingly enough, though, more people are coming down the mountain than going up. Let's take a look at life in the valley and see what we find.

If you picture a valley in your mind, chances are you will find plenty of water running between two mountains – a raging river, a babbling brook, a rapid stream (Revelation 22:17). Where you find water, you find trees that bear fruit (Psalm 1:3). You can hear the wind whispering through the trees as a steady breeze rushes in from the top of the mountain (Acts 2:2). The valley affords shelter and protection from the storms and inclement weather. And even though in the valley the sun shines only for a short period during the day-light hours, we appreciate it that much more when we feel its warmth on our face. The valley is the place where we drink freely of the water and eat freely of the fruit of the trees. Perhaps that is why God does not allow us to settle on the mountaintop for too long.

There are also dangers in the valley that we cannot afford to overlook. Most battles take place on the valley floor. This is the place where the anointed of God meet Goliath. We see this truth manifest in the account of the battle between David and Goliath. Goliath typifies the lust of the flesh, for at some point in our lives we all wanted to be Goliath. A giant among men, Goliath the champion of the Philistines was larger than any man in his day. Given his ability to win battles I can only imagine that Goliath was paraded around and given whatever he desired. In our lust for accomplishment we, too, desire these things in the flesh. To be the champion at what we do, to achieve great success, and to be admired for our natural abilities. You see, until we can defeat our flesh in the valley, we cannot be a man after God's own heart.

We find the account of the battle between David and Goliath in 1 Samuel 17. David, a type of Christ, first goes to the soldiers and asks them about the giant. When no man would dare face the mighty giant, David went to Saul and volunteered to take him on. 1 Samuel 17:32 says, "And David said to Saul, Let no man's heart fail because of him; thy servant will go and fight with this Philistine." Notice that David, being a type of the Lord Jesus Christ, did not have to be asked to defeat the giant. Rather, he volunteered to do so. Saul then tried to suit David up with his own armor, but it would not do. David did not fit into Saul's armor. (We will consider some other lessons this passage teaches regarding Saul's armor in Chapter 10.)

So David went out to do battle with the power of God to protect him and used the weapons that *God* provided for him. Notice what David did in 1 Samuel 17:40. He took five smooth stones out of the brook that ran through the valley. When we find ourselves in the valley facing our Goliath, we need only to rely on what *God* has provided for us. If we go in the power of another man's strength (Saul's armor), we cannot fight the battle and win. Many have considered what these five smooth stones represent (types). As I read through this passage I cannot help but think that David, having spent all that time alone with God tending the sheep, meditated on the word of God that he had heard learned from his father Jesse. As he knelt down by the brook and chose the stones to take with him, I can hear him say as he picked up the first stone, "In the beginning God created the heavens and the earth" (Genesis 1:1). The second stone: "By little and little I will drive them out from before thee" (Exodus 23:30). The third stone: "And he that blasphemeth the name of the LORD, he shall surely be put to death" (Leviticus 24:16). The fourth: "Then ye shall drive out all the inhabitants of the land from before you" (Numbers 33:52). And the fifth and final stone: "And thou shalt love the Lord thy God with all thine heart, and all thy soul, and with all thy might" (Deuteronomy 6:5).

You see, we must face our giants with the word of God and not with weapons of man. We must rely on the Rock of our salvation to slay the giant. Victory over the lusts of the flesh is won in the valley *not* on the mountaintop. God will provide the weapons, the strength for which to fight, and the victory will be His.

The Dry Places of the Desert

Unlike the mountain and the valley, the desert is the place where no glory is found – no springs of water, no trees bearing fruit, and no shelter from the storms. If you have been saved for any length of time, you know of the place I speak. We Christian will go through times in our Christian walk when, seemingly, God is nowhere to be found. The word of God seems void of meaning, our prayers seem to rise no higher than the ceiling, and we find ourselves wandering deliriously through the sands of time in search of an oasis. This is the battlefield known as the lust of the eyes. You see, when we cannot find God our flesh immediately turns to carnal thoughts of provision for the necessities of life and we rely only on what we can see to get us through the day. The scriptures provide us with a perfect picture of this when the children of Israel came up out of Egypt (a type of the world), crossed over the Red sea (a type of salvation), and immediately went into the wilderness. Not long after their journey began they began to murmur and complain (Exodus 14:11-12). They found no water in the wilderness (Exodus 15:22). They found no food in the wilderness (Exodus 16:3). The lesson is simple, really. Proverbs 3:5 says, "Trust in the LORD with all thine heart, and lean not unto thine own understanding" and Philippians 4:19 says, "But my God shall supply all your need according to his riches in glory by Christ Jesus." Trust the Lord and look to *Him* to take care of you. He will lead you through.

When you find yourself in the desert, fear not, for God has not moved, God has not changed, and He still abides on the throne. And seated at the right side of the Father is our Lord and Savior Jesus Christ. He hears your cry and will come to your aid. You need only to look up. As soldiers of Christ, we will fight on this battlefield. God is testing us, proving us. Just as new armor is tested to make sure that it is battle-ready and will endure, so we are tested of God in the desert to see whether we will look *up* or look *back*. The children of Israel continued to look back instead of up. For that, God extended their time in the wilderness for 40 years – 40 being the number of testing in the Bible. My fellow soldier, do not dwell in the wilderness of Sin (Exodus 16:1). Look Up! (Psalm 5:3). Look Up! For your redemption draweth nigh (Luke 21:28).

Inward Battlefields

Courage & Commitment

Regardless of the battlefield on which you find yourself, you will face internal conflicts as well. In every battle, every skirmish, we must find within ourselves courage and commitment. Numbers 13:20 sums up what God expects of us soldiers: "And what the land is, whether it be fat or lean, whether there be wood therein, or not. And be ye of good courage, and bring of the fruit of the land." No matter whether we are in the valley, in the desert, or on the mountaintop, we must find the courage to fight and stand strong.

Few people understand what courage truly is. Courage means simply *the quality of mind and spirit that enables a person to face difficulty or danger.* In addition, courage is *the ability to act in accordance with one's beliefs*. While many would say that those who have courage do not fear, I would say rather that courage is not the absence of fear but rather the self-determination to do what is right and stand strong *in spite of* our fears. Fear is a natural emotion that takes hold of us when faced with challenges outside of our normal comfort zone. Each time God puts a test or trial before us, fear enters our minds. When fear enters our minds, we either stand courageous or we do not.

The Lord recognized this and thus said in Exodus 20:20, "And Moses said unto the people, Fear not: for God is come to prove you, and that his fear may be before your faces, that ye sin not." In Deuteronomy 31:6, as Joshua was just about to lead them into the promised land, Moses told the people, "Be strong and of a good courage, fear not, nor be afraid of them: for the LORD thy God, he it is that doth go with thee; he will not fail thee, nor forsake thee." Understand this: We do not go anywhere or do anything in our own power but only in the power of the Lord Jesus Christ. He has gone before us. In 2 Samuel 5:24 the Bible says, "And let it be, when thou hearest the sound of a going in the tops of the mulberry trees, that then thou shalt bestir thyself: for then shall the LORD go out before thee, to smite the host of the Philistines." Therein lies the great truth that Christian soldiers are to get *stirred up* for the battle.

On February 22, 1991, at 3:00 AM, the call came for our unit to move north through the Saudi desert to the border of Iraq. I recall having mixed emotions at the time – fear being in that mix. My driver and I glanced at each other and I saw in his eyes excitement, fear, and concern. I too was afraid of what we might encounter in the darkness. Moving through the desert during the darkest hours of the night was unsettling to say the least. I half expected to see a flash of light and then dive out of the vehicle and be right in the middle of a battle. My imagination was running wild, and a thousand emotions danced in my mind and body. The driver and I looked at each other and encouraged one another.

Without speaking a word, each of us dredged down deep inside and found that courage and commitment we knew was within. Courage is easier to find when someone beside you is experiencing the same thing (Genesis 2:18). After driving on for about 90 minutes, our convoy stopped. The night still hung dark and heavy upon the desert and we could barely make out our surroundings. My M16 lay in my lap with a hand on the trigger and a thumb on the safety. My other hand gripped the hand-guard and was ready to point and shoot. In that hour and a half I must have checked my side for my other magazines at least 100 times. I remember thinking to myself: *We are just one company and won't last long if we encounter enemy troops of any magnitude.* Our company consisted of 15 tanks, a few Bradley fighting vehicles, a few Personnel Carriers, and a smattering of trucks and Hummers. Not much of a fighting force depending on what we happened upon.

It was sometime between 4:30 and 5:00 AM now. The sky was growing lighter by the minute as the sun began to rise. As I was at last able to start making out the vehicles around us I noticed that we were approaching what seemed to be a large hill directly in front of us. I heard vehicles moving around us, some close and some far off. At some point during the drive, under complete radio silence, we had joined forces with other units moving to the border of Iraq. It was about 5:30 now and the light was streaming over the horizon. I stepped out of the vehicle and look towards the east and noticed that many vehicles had joined our unit. As the sun climbed higher in the morning sky, my heart took courage and so did my driver's.

As far as the eye could see there were US military vehicles of every shape and size. On many a vehicle, I beheld Old Glory flying high and waving proudly in the desert wind – a breathtaking sight that few have beheld and one that is very hard to capture in mere words. We looked at each other again and discovered that our earlier fear and concern had given way to courage and resolve. We BESTIRRED OURSELVES!!! The Bible says, BESTIR THYSELF!!! We are soldiers in a different type of battle now, but the emotions – fear and courage – are just the same. Lives will be won or lost depending on how WE fight!!! BESTIR THYSELF.

*2 Samuel 5:24, "And let it be, when thou hearest the sound of a going in the tops of the mulberry trees, that then thou shalt **bestir thyself**: for then shall the LORD go out before thee, to smite the host of the Philistines."*

Sanctification & Separation

The battlefields we face are our work environment, our family experiences, our church life, the time we spend with God, and the activities we choose to participate in. We can narrow these "theaters" of war down even further to battles and skirmishes such as: how we spend our personal time, how we use the Internet, TV, social gatherings, and work-related events. I recently delivered a sermon at our church regarding our time and how short our lives really are. The Bible says in Psalm 90:10, "The days of our years are threescore years and ten; and if by reason of strength they be fourscore years, yet is their strength labour and sorrow; for it is soon cut off, and we fly away." Eighty years is not a long time. We should take inventory of our time and how we spend it. Although there is nothing wrong with activities and hobbies in and of themselves, they should not replace the gathering of ourselves together with other believers (Hebrews 10:25) or our personal devotion with the Lord.

This message on time resonated with me and several members of our church. God really used this message to convict me about all the time I spend doing things besides serving God. For instance, I am a casual golfer and really love the game. I very much enjoy spending time golfing with my son Tyler. We all need time to unwind and do things we enjoy. I have learned that spending time with my family is second only to time alone with God. They need their father and husband to be there to talk to and share their lives with. As long as we are not replacing our time with God with activities, God gives us liberty to enjoy these types of things as well. We would also do well to find the Lord in those other things that we enjoy. Find God in your hobbies and interests and include Him as you would a good friend. Many of the men in our church love to hunt and fish. As long as we keep the Lord *first* in *all* that we do and do not substitute these activities for time with the Lord, we will do well.

Sin

The following verse describes the sin that every Christian must conquer: the lust of the flesh, the lust of the eyes, and the pride of life (1 John 2:16).

Every sin that we commit falls under one of the categories. The devil used all three when tempting Jesus. He will use all three to tempt you as well. If we are to make any advances for the cause of Christ, we must conquer and defeat the sin that so easily besets us as Hebrews 12:1 tells us: "Wherefore seeing we also are compassed about with so great a cloud of witnesses, let us lay aside every weight, and the sin which doth so easily **beset** us, and let us run with patience the race that is set before us."

Many of us struggle with *how* to get out of the perpetual loop of sin-and-forgiveness, sin-and-forgiveness…. I am reminded of the passage Mark 9:17-29 that culminates with Jesus' saying, "This kind can come forth by nothing, but by prayer and fasting."Take time now to study those verses and ask God to give you victory in this battle! He wants you to have victory!!!

———∞———

"The noblest souls are the most tempted. The devil is a sportsman and likes big game. He makes the deadliest assaults on the richest natures, the finest minds, the noblest spirits."

—John L. Lawrence

———∞———

9

GUARD DUTY

We are all subject to diverse temptations and must constantly be on alert. The devil will stop at nothing to break down our defenses. The greatest power our enemy has is to deceive. We must remain alert and be on guard at all times, just as a soldier in battle who cannot afford to lose focus on the enemy. To help us do this, we will explore two subjects in this chapter:

(1)the need for every Christian to be on alert regarding his or her own testimony, and (2) the need for every Christian to sound the alarm for those who do not or cannot see the enemy coming.

Beware of Pride

Let's look inwardly first. How does the devil deceive us and how do we guard against it? Many of us are deceived daily into thinking more highly of ourselves than we ought to think. Romans 12:3 cautions us against this: "For I say, through the grace given unto me, to every man that is among you, not to think of himself more highly than he ought to think; but to think soberly, according as God hath dealt to every man the measure of faith." The devil is all about pride. Pride is and was in the devil as a roaring lion, as a serpent in the garden, as the anointed cherub that covereth. We see in Ezekiel 28 and Isaiah

14 that pride entered into the heart of Lucifer and he wanted to be like the most high (Isaiah14:14).

We, too, are susceptible to pride and must defend and guard against it every moment of every day. What is pride and what forms does it take? These are questions each one of us must answer for ourselves, for the way pride manifests is unique to each individual. Here are three examples of how pride can begin: when we think someone has done us wrong; when we think we have been cheated out of something we deserve; when we grow discontent with the things that we have. All of these are seeds of pride in our lives (Hebrews 13:5; 1 Timothy 6:8). Just as a soldier whose duty it is to stand as a sentinel at the gate, ever watchful for any sign of an attack, so we must be vigilant as the Bible says in 1 Peter 5:8, "Be sober, be vigilant; because your adversary the devil, as a roaring lion, walketh about, seeking whom he may devour."

On January 30, 1991, for the first time in my military career I was selected for guard duty. Being merely a private first class, I had virtually no sway to pick my guard duty shift. So it was no surprise that I got the graveyard shift – midnight to 3:00 AM. At around 11:30 PM I was woken abruptly to get ready. I brushed off the sand that had settled on me during the night and fumbled around in the dark trying to find my boots and gear. Finally, with boots and Kevlar gear on and M16 in hand, I headed out to the spot where I was to stand for the next three hours. My sergeant met me and gave me the night vision goggles and protocol for the watch as I made my way to my post. I checked my gear to make sure I had water, rifle, and rounds. That was about it. I must admit, I was a little nervous. I was holding a loaded M16 for the first time outside of a firing range and knew that if I had to fire it this time it wouldn't be at a plastic target. Secondly, we were in the middle of the desert with no clearly defined borders. I did not know from which direction an attack might come and so I had to constantly looking in all directions.

The night was so dark that I could barely see my hand in front of my face. The clouds covered the moon and stars, which on most nights lit up the desert as at dawn. My shift began and I stood there…and stood there…and stood there some more. That was the duty, to watch, to peer into the darkness for any sign of the enemy, any sign of anything out of the ordinary. About an hour and a half into the shift, fighting the nods, I found myself walking in circles to stay awake. If you have ever pulled guard duty, you can sympathize. As I walked in circles, I began to feel uneasy, as if someone was coming. I quickly turned on the night vision goggles and held them up to my eyes. I scanned the horizon expecting to see a camel, a truck, a person, something...nothing. The hairs begin to stand up on the back of my neck; my heart was racing like a mad drummer in my chest. The feeling grew stronger. Something was out there! I was fully awake and alert then and hyper-alert when I felt something brush my leg. Had my boots not been strapped on, I would have jumped clear out of them.

In an instant, I drew my weapon, chambered a round, and turned the safety off. I was locked and loaded. Picture me frantically turning one way then the other looking for something to fire at.... Nothing. Again I felt something brush my leg and spun around to see a wild dog running off. *Breathe, Scott.... breathe.* Fortunately for the dog, I had my wits about me and restrained from firing. It took about 10 minutes for my nerves to settle, my heart rate to slow, and my M16 to be put back on SAFE. I was prepared for just about anything – anything, that is, but a dog. It was what I least expected. I was prepared for a column of Iraqi tanks to break the ridge and begin firing on our encampment or a parachute assault from above, but not for a four-legged animal to sneak up on me. I was not prepared for the subtlety of a quiet animal, just as Adam and Eve were not prepared for the subtlety of the serpent in the garden. The moral of the story is this: In spiritual warfare, as in military combat, we may be attacked when least expecting it from a direction we are not watching or in a manner for which we were not prepared.

I was fortunate, had it been something that could do me harm, I would have been caught unawares and become a casualty. Also, my position would have been compromised and our encampment vulnerable. Ponder that for just a minute. If we are to be on constant guard, watching and praying, what hurt does the church of the living God suffer when we fall to a surprise attack of the enemy? Matt 26:41. How long would my position and the area of the encampment been unguarded? The soldiers that are resting from battle are relying on those of us who have been tasked to stand guard. It is our duty to be aware, awake, and alert! Ever watching and praying for the saints of God, our fellow soldiers, and our leaders that they may be strong, that they may fight, that they may advance on the field of battle. It is our responsibility to be able to see in the darkness of this world and recognize the enemy when he is near. We must be vigilant!! Those of us who are selected for guard duty need to have night vision. The interesting thing about night vision goggles is that they only need a small amount of light for the goggles to work perfectly. The basic concept behind night vision goggles is that they gather the light, even a small amount, so that images can be seen in the dark. You see, at night, the moon is the most prominent light source available. The moon only reflects the light of the sun. The moon is a type of the Church. It has no light of its own but reflects the light of the Son. The soldier fighting in the desert places attempting to identify, engage, or defend against the enemy, needs the light of the moon to guide his way and see clearly in the darkest hours. We soldiers take too lightly the purpose of our local churches. Lord forgive us and help us to see clearly in the night hours.

—※—

"…He calleth to me out of Seir, Watchman, what of the night? Watchman, what of the night?"   - Isaiah 21:11

—※—

" . . . *When I bring the sword upon a land, if the people of the land take a man of their coasts, and set him for their watchman: If when he seeth the sword come upon the land, he blow the trumpet, and warn the people; Then whosoever heareth the sound of the trumpet, and taketh not warning; if the sword come, and take him away, his blood shall be upon his own head. He heard the sound of the trumpet, and took not warning; his blood shall be upon him. But he that taketh warning shall deliver his soul. But if the watchman see the sword come, and blow not the trumpet, and the people be not warned; if the sword come, and take any person from among them, he is taken away in his iniquity; but his blood will I require at the watchman's hand.*

- Ezekiel 33:1-6

This passage wakes me up at night. Have I fulfilled my duty? Have I warned those whom God has put in my path? How much of my time have I wasted, and how many have passed by my way but I was too busy to sound the trumpet?

10

WEAPONS AND ARMOR

As soldiers, we are to be fully prepared and fully equipped with our "uniform" before we step onto the battlefield. We cannot neglect one piece of the armor of God. Does a hunter head out to the woods without a rifle or a fisherman to the lake without a basic outfit? Of course not. That would be absurd. Why then do most of us go out to battle without putting on the whole armor of God? I venture to say that it is because most of us do not even realize that we are in a battle. Then some take a few pieces of the armor but not all. Can you imagine getting to your favorite fishing hole and seeing the fish jumping like never before only to realize that you forgot your tackle box? You'll not catch many fish with a bare hook, will you?

So what is the armor of God and why should we put it on? Let's list the pieces so we know exactly what we should have. Ephesians 6:14-17 gives us our uniform and equipment list:

- Loins girt about with truth.

- The breastplate of righteousness.

- Feet shod with the preparation of the gospel of peace.

- Shield of faith.

- The helmet of salvation.

- The sword of the Spirit (which is the word of God).

Then most importantly: "Praying always with all prayer and supplication in the Spirit, and watching thereunto with all perseverance and supplication for all saints," so as to "open my mouth boldly, to make known the mystery of the gospel, for which I am an ambassador in bonds: that therein I may speak boldly, as I ought to speak."

The first thing to notice is the order in which the scripture lists the pieces of armor: They start from the inside and go out. Although that makes practical sense because we usually put on our under garments before our outer garments, let's dig a little deeper to the spiritual meaning of the putting on the armor from the inside out. A great passage in the Old Testament regarding David tells us that God looks on the heart of a man and not on his outward appearance (1 Samuel 16:7). Before going into battle, we must first prepare our heart. All of the armor is spiritual in nature, and thus we must first prepare our innermost man for battle. I have heard many sermons with this theme: "If you get God on the inside, He will fix the outside." Most of us spend hours on end preparing the outward man – tending to our appearance. We start our day with a shower. We shave and style our hair, carefully pick out our clothes, and pamper our flesh for the day ahead. All of us – even the most seasoned veterans – do well to remember that our inner man needs more attention than our outward man. We must start our day bathed in prayer and with reading the word of God to groom our hearts for the day ahead.

Loins girt about with truth

First we start with "having our loins girt about with truth." What is truth? In John 17:17 Jesus says, "Sanctify them through thy truth; thy word is truth." And in John 8:32 He says, "And ye shall know the truth, and the truth shall make you free." In Psalm 119:11 David says, "Thy word have I hid in mine heart, that I might not sin against thee." So by looking at just these three verses of scripture, we start to get the picture of what God is doing in Ephesians 6:11. Having your loins girt about with truth is what enables us to stand. Without going into great detail of human anatomy, our loins are our mid-section (also known as our "core"). The muscles in our mid-section, sides, and lower back are what enables us to stand erect and keep a good posture. Remember the call of Ephesians 6:11 to "stand therefore, having you loins girt about with truth." This means that you are supported by the truth of the word of God.

When I worked in a warehouse I was given a back brace to help support my lower back and mid-section when lifting heavy loads. Some would argue that this only weakens the back muscles and does more harm than good. Be that as it may, a back brace does ensure that you maintain proper posture. During my time in the army, I spent many hours in the gym paying attention to my outward man. A weight belt is an essential piece of equipment for weight lifters. When you are doing squats, the belt which wraps the mid-section and loins, assists in keeping your back straight to avoid muscles pulls and other back injuries. As a soldier of Christ, we will be required to lift heavy loads at times. Having our loins girt about with the truth of the word of God prepares us to manage these loads without injury.

Breastplate of Righteousness

The second piece of armor we soldiers are required to don is the breast-plate of righteousness. It is not hard to envision a breastplate. We have all seen movies of old world soldiers wearing armor. Let's take note of two distinct physical features of the breastplate. First, the breastplate protects the body's most vital organs – chief of which is the heart. A soldier can survive being struck with blows in many part of his anatomy, but blows to the chest or stom-ach are often fatal. The breastplate protects against such wounds.

Let's note that this piece of armor is a *breast*plate and provides little or no protection for the back. A soldier is *never* to retreat or turn his back to the enemy. A soldier is to advance on the field of battle. One of my favorite hymns to sing used to be "Hold the Fort." It is a great hymn, but once I learned that a soldier is not to merely "hold the fort" the song lost its savor. My family will attest that when watching news or commentary on the war in Iraq and Afghanistan, I have said on more than one occasion that soldiers are not the police. I have yet to see a single successful mission in which regular army soldiers are used to "keep the peace." A soldier is trained to fight, to advance, to pursue, and to inflict damage on the enemy. I was never trained to fire only when fired upon. I was trained to identify the enemy and *fire!* It is sad to say that most Christians have taken up a defensive position and a peace-keeping effort (which is different from peace-*making*). Brother, our enemy will not rest. He will not cease to launch his arrows. He does not want peace. He wants to destroy you! Souls will not be won by holding the fort. Souls will be one only by advancing on the field of battle.

Above the baptistery in a church we once belonged to hung an old rugged cross with a crown of thorns set on it. We moved out of state, but several years later we happened upon some pictures of the sanctuary of our old church and discovered that the crown of thorns had been removed from atop the cross. We asked some old friends what had happened to the crown and were sorry to hear that the church's new pastor had taken it down for fear that it might offend someone. My wife and looked at each other and pondered why a crown of thorns in a Christian church would offend anyone. To this day I cannot answer that question. This is most assuredly the gospel of peace – that He suffered and died for our sins. What great peace I received in my heart once I accepted the Lord Jesus Christ as my savior. You see, the gospel of peace is not that we preach peace but rather that we preach Christ, the Prince of Peace, who is the One who gives peace to those who accept Him as Savior. To have your feet shod with the preparation of the gospel of peace is to preach Christ crucified and risen again the third day.

Sadly, many Christians have become apathetic in their daily lives. Our churches are plagued with a type of spiritual lethargy. We do not want to "offend" anyone. I am by no means suggesting that we go out of our way to offend others. I am merely stating that the Word of God, preached and taught as it is written, will offend the lost. It is supposed to do so. The Lord Jesus Christ offended more people than any of us ever will. Did He set out to offend simply for the sake of doing so? No. But the truth of the words that He spoke by nature were contrary to their carnal nature (Romans 8:7). In essence we have retreated. We have turned our back to our enemy, who has launched a massive attack on our churches that has wounded countless soldiers and weakened us. Even worse, those of us who have survived or fought our way back often look down on those who have fallen and wag our heads.

Now that we have explored the physical aspect of the breastplate, let's look at its spiritual characteristics. It is a breastplate of *righteousness*. Recently, I was leading the youth of our church through a verse-by-verse study of the first chapter of Hebrews. Verse 8 mentions the "sceptre of righteousness." We paused for a time to really understand what righteousness means. The root word of righteousness is righteous. I challenged the youth to really understand what it means to be right with God.

To understand a word's intended meaning in the Bible, it is good to explore the first time it occurs in scripture. Many times, the context in which it is first used will be the context intended throughout the rest of the Bible. Our study took us back to Genesis 7:1, the first time the word righteous occurs in the Bible. The reference is to Noah's being found righteous in God's eyes as the reason God saved Noah and his family. So, if we want to know what it means to be righteous, we must look at the story of Noah and note how he walked with God. He separated himself from a wicked world. We, too, are to be different, a peculiar people (1 Peter 2:9). We are to be obedient to God and live our lives in a manner that brings Him glory and honor. Of course, we can also simply look at the testimony of the Lord and those things written in the gospels. To be a Christian is to be Christ-like and to live a righteous life. Doing so will protect your heart. Not doing so will leave you venerable to attack.

Feet shod with the preparation of the gospel of peace

One of the most important parts of the armor is the shoes. Soldiers trained to guard prisoners are taught to make sure that they are barefoot. Their shoes are stripped off so they cannot run quickly in the event they escape. Any POW will verify this. The devil would like nothing more than to have us shoeless.

How are we to run our race without the shoes we are given? I enjoy running and my favorite article of clothing is a new pair of running shoes. Good running shoes are light (Matthew 11:30). Boots are an important part of the soldier's apparel. Soldiers are required to march many miles at a time. Any soldier will testify that a good pair of boots makes a world of difference on a road march.

When I was in basic training during an eight-mile road march I developed an ingrown toenail because I was wearing boots half a size too small. It was quite possibly the most excruciating pain I had felt up to that point in my life. At the halfway point we stopped briefly to change our socks and my drill sergeant noticed my big toe was bleeding. It was numb at that point, and I seriously did not want to ride on the back of the truck while the rest of my company finished the road march. I convinced the drill sergeant to let me keep going and lasted about another two miles before he made me ride out the rest of the march. This experience illustrates an important point: My lack of proper preparation jeopardized the mission because the rest of the company had to slow down and adjust the pace to accommodate my injury.

So the Bible tells us to have our feet shod (covered) with the preparation of the gospel of peace. We are to be prepared to give an answer to every man of the hope that lies within us (1 Peter 3:15). We are to prepare daily for the battle. As a young preacher – in experience not age – I have recently learned a valuable lesson. My pastor told me that regardless of what text you draw your message from, it should always end at the cross. In his words, "Pick a scripture and make a beeline to the cross." Listen to Christian radio and note how many "sermons" leave out the death, burial, and resurrection of the Lord Jesus Christ. These sermons will not draw sinners to Christ. I have heard men preach great messages with illustrations that I could never think of only to leave out the most important part – Christ crucified and risen again. Although every Bible lesson does not center on the cross, I can find barely a scripture in the Bible that does not lend itself, in some manner, to the story of the cross, which is the grand theme over the scriptures: the sacrifice of our Lord for our souls. I challenge you to look for Christ in every passage of scripture. As I tell my class often, the Old Testament is pointing us to the cross and the New Testament is the reflection of the cross. All scripture is centered on Christ.

Shield of faith

Next we will explore the shield of faith. What is faith? Hebrews 11:1 defines it this way: "Now faith is the substance of things hoped for, the evidence of things not seen." That clears it up, right? Not exactly. Faith is simply this – believing what you cannot see and believing what God said about the things you cannot see. In the Old Testament, God appeared to His people and left no doubt as to what they were supposed to do. Most often, they heard it directly from the mouth of the Lord or from an angel of the Lord. I have often thought that if God would just audibly tell me exactly what He wanted me to do, I would do it. But then where would faith be? If we could see God and hear God, why would we need faith?

We need only look to "doubting Thomas" for an illustration of faith and sight. John 20:26-31 recounts how Christ, after His resurrection, appeared to the disciples when Thomas was among them. When Jesus had first appeared to His disciples after the resurrections and before His ascension, Thomas was elsewhere. Thomas was doubtful and declared that he would not believe unless he saw the Lord himself. In verse 29 we read: "Jesus saith unto him, Thomas, because thou hast seen me, thou has believed: blessed are they that have not seen, yet have believed."

So we are to take the shield of faith, believing the word of God and the testimony of the men and women who did see Him, and join those eyewitnesses in believing in Him. Personally I have never found it difficult to believe that God exists and that He created and upholds all things by the word of His power (Hebrews 1:3). What evidence do we have that these things are so? The evidence is all around us. We see it every day and night. In Psalms 19:1 God says, "The heavens declare the glory of God; and the firmament sheweth his handywork." Most of us stop right there. But God in His infinite wisdom added two more verses to drive home the fact that no human being is incapable of seeing these things and believing on the Lord. Psalms 19:2-3 says, "Day unto day uttereth speech and night unto night sheweth knowledge. There is no speech nor language, where their voice is not heard." What uttereth speech? What sheweth knowledge? Why the heavens and the firmament mentioned in verse 1. Look closely at verse 3, which declares that their voice is heard all throughout the world. This is the evidence of things not seen referred to in Hebrews 11:1.

So how do we get faith with which to defend ourselves against the fiery darts of the devil? Let us look at Romans 10:17: "so then faith cometh by hearing, and hearing by the word of God." To increase in faith we need only to listen. Listen to what? The word of God. Each time we hear the word of God taught, preached, or read our faith is increased. You might be saying to yourself, "I can only go to church three times a week, so how can I increase my faith with only about four hours a week of listening?"

Here's how. There are many audio readings of the Bible on the market, including the wonderful version read by Alexander Scourby. These audio Bibles are available in MP3 format so you can listen to them on any MP3 player. They are also available in CD and cassette tape formats. Thus, anyone can listen to the word of God on the way to work each day, while jogging or working out, or while falling asleep at night. In addition, you can always read aloud to yourself. I have heard many preachers say that this is the preferred method of Bible reading. You not only see and speak the word but also hear it. Using all three senses at one time will help you absorb and remember what you have read. Psalms 119:11 says, "Thy word have I hid in mine heart, that I might not sin against thee."

- To live by faith is a requirement of the Christian life.

- No one can come to the Lord except by faith.

- There is no way to please the Father except by faith.

—C. Sexton

"While we look not at the things which are seen, but at the things which are not seen: for the things which are seen are temporal; but the things which are not seen are eternal."

-2 Corinthians 4:18

The helmet of salvation

In the army we were required to wear a Kevlar helmet when on training exercises and on duty in Saudi Arabia and Iraq. Soldiers despise no part of the battle dress uniform more than that Kevlar helmet. It is heavy and awkward. It rarely fits well, and the chin strap grates on the chin and causes discomfort. But, then again, if you have ever been in war and had shots fired directly at you, you probably do not feel the same way about that helmet. I was fortunate never to have had a bullet fired directly at me either in training or in the Gulf.

Let's consider the necessity of a helmet for a soldier. The helmet protects the head and brain from injuries from bullets and shrapnel while in battle. A significant head wound is most often fatal – or, at the very least, brings devastating debilitation. We've all heard the stories of people who suffered a head wound in which the penetrating object lodged so perfectly between the two hemispheres of the brain that it did not cause any damage to the brain and the person survived. This is the exception. Most who suffer a head wound do not survive.

Spiritually, the helmet of salvation protects our thoughts and mind. The devil attacks our thoughts with wickedness on a daily basis. Everywhere we look while going about our daily lives, we are tempted with evil thoughts and pictures of sin at every turn. You can hardly drive two miles down the road without seeing a billboard saturated with sin. The Bible says that God knows our every thought. In the book of Job, God rebuked Job for his self-righteousness saying, "Behold, I know your thoughts, and the devices which ye wrongfully imagine against me" (Job 21:27). Psalms 94:11 confirms this when David says, "The LORD knoweth the thoughts of man, that they are vanity."

As always, the Lord has provided us soldiers of Christ with the means to overcome the wicked thoughts of our heart and mind. He has given us a piece of spiritual armor – the helmet of salvation – designed specifically to protect us from the thoughts that the devil tries to put into our heads. Remember, this is a spiritual battle and the enemy's goal is to render us ineffective for Christ. For new believers, very often the thought that runs through your head is doubt regarding your salvation. Once we have repented of our sin (nature) and accepted Christ as our savior, the devil begins putting doubts in our head so that we fear that we are not saved. This is effective in large measure because even after we are saved we still continue to commit sins (acts against God) for which we must ask forgiveness. Know this, soldier: You were not saved because of your works and you are not kept saved because of your works (Ephesians 2:8). For seasoned Christians, the devil most often attacks our thoughts with those sins that, as the Apostle Paul put it, "so easily beset us" (Hebrews 12:1).

So how do both young and seasoned Christians overcome this attack? Once again, God has provided the answer for us in Proverbs 16:3: "Commit thy works unto the LORD, and thy thoughts shall be established." If we are to overcome the attack on our thoughts, we must commit ourselves to God daily. You may be wondering why it is called the helmet of *salvation*, especially if you do not doubt your salvation. Why the emphasis on salvation and our thought life? That is a good question that deserves a good answer. The helmet is not for *your* salvation but for the salvation of *others*. There is no greater way to "commit thy works unto the LORD" than to be a continual witness for Jesus Christ. You see, if your works are committed to God and you are always thinking, praying, and speaking about our Lord and savior and asking Him to save the souls of those around you, the devil will have a hard time putting evil thoughts in your head (1 Thessalonians 5:17).

Remember, the helmet of salvation protects our thoughts and our mind. We discussed our thoughts, so now let's focus on our mind. Our thoughts are those individual occurrences that come and go. Our mind is somewhat more detailed. It is the part of us that reasons and that has a purpose, intent, and will. Philippians 2:5 says, "Let this mind be in you, which was also in Christ Jesus." In the next few verses of this passage we find that Christ humbled Himself and became obedient to the death of the cross. Later on, the passage tells us to "work out our salvation with fear and trembling." We are instructed to do all things without murmurings and disputing so that we may be blameless, harmless, without rebuke "in the midst of a crooked and perverse nation, among whom ye shine as lights in the world … holding forth the word of life." This is the mind of Christ (read the entire passage, Philippians 2:5-17).

Let's list the qualities of the mind of Christ again so that we don't get lost in the passage: Humble; obedient; do all things without murmuring or disputing; blameless; harmless; holding fast the word of life; and shining as a light in the world. As you can see, the helmet of salvation is much more than mere protection for our heads. The helmet is to protect us from the devil and his attack on our thoughts and mind. We put on the helmet by keeping our thoughts and minds focused on Jesus Christ and on the salvation of others. We must start each day focusing our minds on Christ.

I want to share another passage that has helps me immensely, Philippians 4:7-8: "And the peace of God, which passeth all understanding, shall keep your hearts and minds through Christ Jesus. Finally, brethren, whatsoever things are true, whatsoever things *are* honest, whatsoever things *are* just, whatsoever things *are* pure, whatsoever things *are* lovely, whatsoever things *are* of good report; if *there be* any virtue, and if *there be* any praise, think on these things."

The sword of the Spirit (which is the word of God)

The army trains soldiers to use many different types of weapons. One particular weapon, however, is common to every soldier – the rifle. The M16 (A1&A2) was the rifle used when I was enlisted. Every soldier was required to train and qualify on it at least once every six months. Even if the primary weapon assigned to a soldier was something other than the M16, the soldier still had to qualify with this weapon first. Here's why. On the modern battlefield, do you have mostly officers with 9MMs or soldiers with M16s? You better have more soldiers with M16s than officers with side-arms or you'll be in sore trouble when confronting the enemy. Even officers know that the M16 is a more effective weapon than a 9MM. What do you think would happen if you lost your own weapon and then picked up a weapon that you had never used from a wounded soldier? You would not be very effective with that weapon and would likely become a casualty yourself. The weapon of choice of those mighty men mentioned in the Old Testament was the sword. Sure, they used spears and bows, but at a minimum every soldier was armed with a sword.

Likewise, every Christian soldier has a sword and some even have arrows (Psalm 127:4-5). Now our swords and arrows are not carnal but spiritual. The verse that best describes the sword of the Spirit is Hebrews 4:12: "For the word of God is quick, and powerful, and sharper than any two-edged sword, piercing even to the dividing asunder of soul and spirit, and of the joints and marrow, and is a discerner of the thoughts and intents of the heart." Hebrews 4:12 is quite a mouthful but lists characteristics of the word of God: It is quick, powerful, and sharper than any two-edged sword. Its purpose is to discern the thoughts and intents of the heart by piercing even the dividing asunder of soul and spirit and joints and morrow. Let's take a closer look at these three characteristics of our weapon of choice.

The word of God is quick. This is not a reference to speed but rather to life. The word of God is *alive*. It is a living document that can be applied to every situation, every person, and every need. Have you ever wondered why, when you need it most, God reveals something to you out of His word that meets the need for the moment that you are in? It is because the Bible was written by the hand of God. It also has the ability to bring life. Ephesians 2:1 says, "And you hath he quickened, who were dead in trespasses and sins." For those of us who have accepted the Lord Jesus Christ as our personal savior, He has made us alive!

The word of God is powerful. I am always amazed at the power the word of God has when it is quoted correctly. If you have ever quoted a passage of scripture in a group of unbelievers, you know that the word of God brings a hush to the conversation. Every mouth is stopped and every thought, if only for a brief moment, is focused on the words of God. Every being, saved or unsaved, must yield to the power of God's word. This should come as no surprise to us given that Genesis 1:1 tells us that "In the beginning God created the heavens and the earth." How did God create the heavens and the earth? He *spoke* it into existence. Genesis 1:3 says, "And God said...." Verse 1:6 says, "And God said...." So God spoke the earth and the heavens into existence.

We have no trouble believing these scriptures. Look outside and see the creation of God. His words emanate from the creation. Psalms 19:1-3 says, "The heavens declare the glory of God; and the firmament sheweth his handywork. Day unto day uttereth speech, and night unto night sheweth knowledge. There is no speech nor language, where their voice is not heard." The creation uttereth speech, and there is no place on earth where the words of God through the creation are not heard! If that is not convincing enough (and it must not have been) God saw fit to record 66 books through many different writers and put them together for us so that we might know His words. Amen! The word of God has the power to stop us in our tracks and make us listen, if only for a moment, to what God has said and is saying.

The word of God is sharper than any two-edged sword. Just by the description alone, we can see that there are two edges to the word of God. The word of God has the power to save and the power to destroy. Every time you hear the word of God you *must* make a decision. Believer or unbeliever, you *must* make a decision. There is no variableness with God (James 1:17). God is no respecter of persons (Acts 10:34). The two edges refer to the decision that must be made when one is presented with the word of God: yea or nay; accept or reject; saved or lost.

We've discussed briefly that the word of God is alive, powerful, and decisive but to what end?

The How

"piercing even to the dividing asunder of soul and spirit, and of the joints and marrow, and is a discerner of the thoughts and intents of the heart."

The "how" of the sword (the word of God) is that it divides asunder the soul, spirit, and body (joints and morrow). To fully expose the reality of what takes place in someone who accepts the Lord Jesus Christ would require a book in itself. A detailed exposition of exactly how this happens would require an in-depth study into the physical and spiritual nature and eternity. That level of detail is beyond the scope of this book, but I do recommend that you explore this topic of study and discuss it with your pastor. Suffice it to say that the word of God has the power to quicken (make alive) your spirit and save your soul from eternal damnation (Ephesians 2:1; 1 Peter 1:9; James 1:21).

The Work

Lastly, we see that the word of God is a discerner of the thoughts and intents of the heart. We read in 1 Chronicles 28:9 that "the LORD searcheth all hearts." We Christians know that God deals with the matters of our heart. We know that when our heart is not right and we have iniquity in our heart the word of God searches those things out and speaks against them. You see, God wants our hearts to be pure and our thoughts to be on Him. He has given us His word so that we can know our own heart.

Another aspect of the "two-edged" sword is that it can be used as both an offensive and a defensive weapon. As an offensive spiritual weapon, the word of God will search out that iniquity in the hearts of the lost and bring them to a place of decision. As a defensive weapon, the word of God rebukes the devil. Notice how the Lord Jesus rebuked Satan when He was tempted. He rebuked him with scripture: "Then saith Jesus unto him, Get thee hence, Satan: for **it is written**, Thou shalt worship the Lord thy God, and him only shalt thou serve" (Matthew 4:10). We would do well to do the same thing when faced with temptation. David said in Psalms 119:11, "Thy word have I hid in mine heart, that I might not sin against thee." From a defensive perspective, the best way to use our sword is to memorize scripture. In 2 Timothy 4:2 we are told to "preach the word; be instant in season, out of season; reprove, rebuke, exhort with all longsuffering and doctrine." This scripture is primarily used by preachers for preachers, but we all preach the word when we witness, when we exalt the Lord, and when we quote scripture as a defense against the wiles of the devil.

Although we have by no means exhausted the descriptions and practical uses of the armor of God, we have examined the armor and should now have a better understanding of what each piece is and why and how we need to be prepared. Remember that we cannot fight for the Lord on the battlefield if we are half dressed for battle. We must put on the whole armor of God (Ephesians 6:11). Each piece of armor serves a specific purpose in both our defensive and our offensive positions as Christians. Remember what we have discussed in the earlier chapters.

We Christian soldiers are to advance on the battlefield. We must also remember that we are not in this fight alone. We are in this fight with other soldiers. They, too, must don the armor of God, the *whole* armor of God. Remember that it is our duty as fellow soldiers to look out for one another, check each other's gear, and make sure that we are fit to fight. We should not do this with a haughty spirit but in loving kindness as Christ has done for us. Our Lord and Savior did not speak down to us and judge us but rather has been longsuffering with grace and mercy. We are to follow His example when helping other soldiers prepare for battle (John 15:12).

Recall that great truth of 1 Samuel 17: We cannot fight with another man's armor. It didn't work for David when Saul tried to outfit him with his own armor, and it will certainly not work for us.

Prayer

"Praying always with all prayer and supplication in the Spirit, and watching thereunto with all perseverance and supplication for all saints" (Ephesians 6:18)

The armor without prayer is useless. The single most important activity we perform as soldiers is prayer. It is responsible for more victories on the field of battle than any other activity. Search the Old Testament scriptures and you will find that whenever the people of God sought out God and His approval, they found victory. Then contrast that with those times when they either did not seek the Lord's direction or ignored it (King Saul) with disastrous results. Our Lord and Savior desires to have communion with His children. From the very beginning, He has sought a relationship with us. He desires to have a relationship and fellowship with us. Pray always, pray without ceasing, pray, pray, pray....

"And the Lord God called unto Adam, and said unto him, where art thou?"- Genesis 3:9

11

UNDER FIRE

A lmost immediately the 1st Armored Division was called upon to meet a new challenge. In November 1990, it was alerted for deployment to the Middle East in
response to the Iraqi invasion of Kuwait. In less than two months the Division moved
17,400 soldiers and 7,050 pieces of equipment by rail, sea, and air to Saudi Arabia
for Operations Desert Shield and Desert Storm. The Division's own 1st Brigade stayed
in Germany and was replaced by 3rd Brigade, 3rd Infantry Division. On 24 February
1991, the 1st Armored Division crossed into Iraq, leading VII Corp's main flanking
attack. Its mission was to destroy the elite Iraqi Republican Guards Divisions. In its
89-hour blitz across the desert Old Ironsides traveled 250 kilometers; destroyed 768
tanks, APCs and artillery pieces; and captured 1,064 prisoners of war. Four 1st Armored
Division soldiers made the ultimate sacrifice in this historic effort. Old Ironsides marked
its successful return to Germany on 8 May 1991, when Major General Griffith uncased
the Division Colors in Ansbach. The 1st Armored Division celebrated its triumph with a
visit from the Vice President of the United States and attendance at victory parades in
Washington, DC and New York City.——Source Unknown

I recall the very moment in Iraq when we had crossed the berm and
advanced forward to engage the enemy. Although I was focused on the task at
hand, my thoughts drifted into "what if" land. *What if* the soldiers ahead were
overrun and we had to face the enemy head on? We mechanics were adequately
trained for direct combat but spent most of our time studying repair and field

recovery techniques rather than in direct combat. My mind raced with different scenarios and how I would react. I remember distinctly checking my M16, my ammo, and my NBC mask. Then: *What if* we were hit by indirect fire from both friendly forces and enemy forces? There was so much talk about SCUD missiles at the time that I half expected to see one hurtling over the horizon any minute. The *thought* of war is certainly more glorious than the *act* of war. We Americans have commercialized war and are so inundated with Hollywood war movies that we have glorified it into something that it is not.

Most soldiers will tell you that an adequate amount of mental preparation occurs before battle, but when the moment comes to advance or engage the enemy, a switch clicks! Fight or flight! Most soldiers rise to the occasion and fight. Our freedom and security depend on it. Whether you agree with the political reasons or motivations behind the war or not, most of us root for our soldiers on the field of battle.

Every Christian young and old is faced with a similar challenge. Unfortunately, my experience tells me that most choose "flight" instead of "fight." This chapter is for those who fight. Every Christian soldier actively engaged in battle will come under direct and indirect fire. Most of the fire will come from our family members or those with whom we work. Most of us have come under attack in the workplace. While stationed at Ft. Knox, I distinctly recall the soldiers' referring to me as "preacher" and mocking me for what I stood for and believed. Most thought I was naive. I chuckled inside and just thanked the Lord that He had washed away the vile testimony I once had and replaced it with a clean slate, as white as snow (Isaiah 1:18). While most of them did not mean any harm by the remarks, some did. This is just one way that a Christian soldier will come under indirect fire. In Matthew 5:10 Jesus says, "Blessed are they which are persecuted for righteousness' sake: for theirs is the kingdom of heaven." Please understand that I do not consider anything that I have experienced as persecution!

In his preaching Pastor Don Mangus used to say often, "Don't wear your feelings on your sleeve." I recall this saying whenever a co-worker makes a comment regarding my stand for the Lord. What type of soldier would I be if I retreated every time I came under fire? Very few battles would be won for the Lord. How we react when faced with indirect or direct fire reveals our character and our courage. So what should our reaction be? Paul says in 1 Corinthians 4:12, "And labour, working with our own hands: being reviled, we bless; being persecuted, we suffer it." Suffer it. It is not difficult to suffer a comment. The apostles were beaten for their stand. Many throughout history have suffered far greater persecution than we face today. The Bible says that this world is not our home; we are pilgrims and strangers in a land that is not ours. You see, when we release our grip on this world, the world and those around us will have little impact on us.

So what are some ways to protect against attack? There is absolutely no way to avoid conflict in Christian warfare.....Actually, I retract that last statement. There is one sure way to guarantee that you are not attacked – live as a carnal Christian. Live as you did before you were saved and the devil will leave you be. The trouble is, God will as well. Any soldier preparing for battle will prepare himself beforehand. We spend countless hours doing physical training exercises to prepare our bodies. Every Sunday School teacher and preacher I have ever known has underscored the importance of preparing yourself in the morning. Finding time for prayer and for reading. The objective is to get battle-ready so that in that moment when the battle is hot and you are under fierce attack you can stand. How do you make sure that retreat or falling to the enemy is not an option and that you do not expose your back to the enemy or become a POW?

A Three-Point Plan When Under Attack: Quote Scripture, Pray, and Sing

I have found that three practices help us overcome the "moment." The first is to *quote scripture*. Any scripture will do. If you have a verse or passage committed to memory that applies specifically to the moment, praise the Lord! If not, remember that your enemy, the devil, hates all scripture, especially those that speak specifically of glorifying the Savior. Your daily devotion should consist of memorizing scripture or at least reciting it over and over. I would recommend starting with committing one verse of scripture to memory each week.

The second is to *pray*. Whether I pray aloud or to myself depends on the situation. When I am being tempted with sin, I find a place to get down on my knees or bow my head and just ask for *Help!* If I am being faced with a situation at work or a person is speaking directly to me, I just start asking the Lord to remove the situation or defuse it. Both in the manufacturing industry and in my days as a soldier in the US Army, I have found myself at times in conversations or meetings where the topic turns south quickly. Although most people who realize that you are a Christian will show some level of respect for it, a few do not. It seems the higher up in the organization or chain of command you go, the worse it gets. So I pray. I pray that the *Lord* would change the subject. I pray that the *Lord* would give me patience. In some cases, I simply have to tell the offending parties to please watch their mouth or I will have to leave the room. Most of the time, the Lord takes care of it. I have watched many an executive choke and cough on water or nothing at all after making a snide comment or uttering something inappropriate.

Lastly, *sing*. When things get stressful at work or at home, and the load seems too heavy to bear, I sing! I have heard it said a hundred times that the devil hates a singing Christian. Every Christian ought to own a hymnbook and memorize some of the old hymns. Though I enjoy some of the newer songs about the Lord, there is nothing like an old hymn about our crucified and risen Savior to put my mind at ease, give me peace within, and stir my soul for the work of the Lord. One of my all-time favorites is *Deeper than the Stain has Gone*.

DEEPER THAN THE STAIN HAS GONE

♪ Dark the stain that soiled man's nature, Long the distance that he fell.
♪ Far removed from hope and heaven, Into deep despair and hell.
♪ But there was a fountain opened, And the blood of God's own Son,
♪ Purifies the soul and reaches Deeper than the stain has gone!

> **Chorus**
> Praise the Lord for full salvation,
> God still reigns upon His throne.
> And I know the blood still reaches
> Deeper than the stain has gone.

♪ Conscious of the deep pollution, Sinners wander in the night,
Tho' they hear the Shepherd calling, They still fear to face the light.
♪ This the blessed consolation, That can melt the heart of stone,
♪ That sweet Balm of Gilead reaches Deeper than the stain has gone!

♪ All unworthy we who've wandered, And our eyes are wet with tears;
♪ As we think of love that sought us Through the weary wasted years.
♪ Yet we walk the holy highway, Walking by God's grace alone
♪ Knowing Calvary's fountain reaches Deeper than the stain has gone!

♪ When with holy choirs we're standing, In the presence of the King,
♪ And our souls are lost in wonder, While the white robed choirs sing;
♪ Then we'll praise the name of Jesus, With the millions round the throne;
♪ Praise Him for the power that reaches, Deeper than the stain has gone!

—Adger McDavid Pace (1882-1959)

Crucified with Christ

We would do well to remember Galatians 2:20: "I am crucified with Christ: nevertheless I live; yet not I, but Christ liveth in me: and the life which I now live in the flesh I live by the faith of the Son of God, who loved me, and gave himself for me."

If I am crucified with Christ, there are several things I cannot do. I cannot stray because I am affixed to the cross. I cannot provide for myself because my arms and legs are affixed to the cross. Finally, I cannot look behind me. The first two will prove out my faith because I am relying on the Lord 100% to take care of all my needs and to keep me. The last is most important to me and will likely be so to those who were not saved as a child or who strayed afterwards. If I am crucified with Christ, I cannot look behind. The devil will not be able to "remind" me of the sin I had in my life before I was saved. The devil will attempt to do this to discredit you. He will try to discredit you and ruin your testimony to those around you, but mostly he will discourage you by telling you that you are worthless and undeserving. When the devil tries this tactic on me, I simply remind him that he is absolutely 100% correct. I am not worthy of the love God showed towards me. But while I was yet in my sin, Christ died for me. Then I remind the old wicked one of these verses:

Romans 5:6:"For when we were yet without strength, in due time Christ died for the ungodly."

Romans 5:8:"But God commendeth his love toward us, in that, while we were yet sinners, Christ died for us."

1 Corinthians 15:3:"For I delivered unto you first of all that which I also received, how that Christ died for our sins according to the scriptures."

Then I remind the devil that my sins are gone forever more, cast in the deepest sea, removed as far as the East is from the West (Psalms 103:12; Micah 7:19).

Give First Aid to the Wounded

One of the basic fundamentals every soldier learns is how to apply first aid to a fellow soldier who is wounded or injured in battle. In basic training, we learned how to evaluate a casualty and apply the appropriate first aid. Most often, first aid and the steps taken in the first few minutes can save a soldier's life. In order to administer first aid, we must be aware of what is going on around us and of those who may have sustained wounds so that we can apply treatment. My wife and I were talking the other day about our church in Kentucky. We were both in our mid-20s and on fire for the Lord. We were involved in everything we could get involved in because we simply loved being around and enjoyed the fellowship with God's people. For several years, I was involved in the prison ministry, the street preaching ministry, and taught 5th grade Sunday school. I was so busy that I did not notice that some members of our church were falling away. My wife Lisa is not one to talk about others' issues and did not say anything to me until I inquired as to their whereabouts. We left Kentucky in 1999 and moved back to Arizona after my enlistment in the Army was complete. It was only then that I realized that our church had suffered many casualties. Some were minor flesh wounds and others were mortal. We need to make sure that we do not leave other wounded soldiers on the field of battle. We need also to make sure that we are adequately prepared for battle so we do not become casualties ourselves when we come under fire. Today, it seems the battlefield is full of casualties – so much so that many preachers and full-time ministers spend much of their time tending to the wounded that the banner of the cross suffers little or no advancement.

Stand Strong

As a conclusion to this chapter, I would like to remind us all that we shall suffer persecution.

2 Timothy 3:12: "Yea, and all that will live godly in Christ Jesus shall suffer persecution."

I dare say that we have not nor will we suffer persecution like that of the early church. There may come a day before the Lord returns, however, when we will be physically persecuted for our faith. Until then, I remind myself that I have not much to cry about. I have in my library a volume titled *Book of Martyrs* (pre-dating Foxe's Book of Martyrs) that I picked up from His Book Store in Brown County, Indiana. This 540-page book recounts in detail the martyrdom of Christians like you and me who were physically persecuted, tortured, and killed for their faith. I will not go into detail regarding the specific methods of persecution, some of which I have not and probably will not finish reading because they are simply too painful and graphic even to read. Reading just a few pages of this book is usually enough to get me to quit my whining and remind myself to stop being a sissy and STAND STRONG.

———

"Wherefore take unto you the whole armour of God, that ye may be able to withstand in the evil day, and having done all, to stand. Stand therefore."

- Ephesians 6:13-14

———

12

HOW TO BE SAVED

The Bible clearly states that you "must be born again." It is very simple to be saved and takes only a minute to explain. Please let me share with you from the Bible, God's word, exactly how to get to heaven from the Bible.

First, every person must understand that he or she is a sinner.

Romans 3:10: *"As it is written, There is none righteous, no, not one."*

Romans 3:23: *"For all have sinned, and come short of the glory of God."*

Second, there is a price that must be paid for our sin, and that price is eternal death in Hell.

Romans 6:23: *"For the wages of sin is death; but the gift of God is eternal life through Jesus Christ our Lord."*

Romans 5:12: *"Wherefore, as by one man sin entered into the world, and death by sin; and so death passed upon all men, for that all have sinned."*

Revelation 20:15: *"And whosoever was not found written in the book of life was cast into the lake of fire."*

The best news of all is that Jesus, God's Only Begotten Son, paid the price by dying on the cross and shedding His blood for our sins.

Romans 5:8: *"But God commendeth his love toward us, in that, while we were yet sinners, Christ died for us."*

John 3:16: *"For God so loved the world, that he gave his only begotten Son, that whosoever believeth in him should not perish, but have everlasting life."*

1 Timothy 1:15: *"This is a faithful saying, and worthy of all acceptation, that Christ Jesus came into the world to save sinners; of whom I am chief."*

We can be saved by Faith in Jesus Christ and what He did on the cross and by Him alone. Salvation is not found in our works of righteousness or in religion but only in THE PERSON OF THE LORD JESUS CHRIST.

John 11:25: *"Jesus said unto her, I am the resurrection, and the life: he that believeth in me, though he were dead, yet shall he live."*

John 14:6: *"Jesus saith unto him, I am the way, the truth, and the life: no man cometh unto the Father, but by me."*

Romans 10:13: *"For whosoever shall call upon the name of the Lord shall be saved."*

CALL UPON THE LORD JESUS CHRIST

Admit that you are a sinner guilty before God.

Believe that Jesus is the Son of God and died on the cross and shed His sinless blood for your sin.

Ask Jesus to forgive you of your sin and accept Him as your personal Savior.

If you see your need for salvation now, simply pray to God a prayer something like the one below. Saying the prayer does not save you; the Lord Jesus saves you because you believe this truth in your heart and ask Him to save you.

Dear Jesus,

I know that I am a sinner. I believe that the punishment for this sin is eternity in Hell. I believe in my heart that You shed Your blood for my sins and rose again the third day. I ask You to forgive me, be my personal Savior, and save my soul from Hell. In Jesus' name, Amen.

If you accepted the Lord Jesus Christ as your personal savior just now, I'd love for you to send me an email at scottharrison@hpgministries.com.

CONCLUSION

As soldiers of the cross, we are looked upon from every direction. This includes our children, our parents, our extended family, co-workers, and strangers alike. The lost world looks at us Christians and makes a determination as to whether they will give consideration to what we say or dismiss us based on our action, attitude, and accountability. My prayer is that this book has helped you and that you will reflect on the suggestions, instructions, and recommendations often as you fight the good fight. May God richly bless you in all that you do and may souls be saved as a result. For there is no other calling greater than leading souls to our Savior, The Lord Jesus Christ. All glory and honor belongs to Him and Him alone.

Coming soon

Return Ye Children of Men

This work is a look at creation all the way to the cross. Spending time looking at the purpose of God's Plan for sinners before the foundation of the world and an "unseen" perspective on the events recorded in the scriptures.

Many Christians simply read the text as a story book and neglect to understand and apply a real life understanding of what was taking place between the lines. *"And God saw that his work was good and God rested on the seventh day."* The dawn of creation strikes me as a time filled with awesome wonder. As put by A. W. Tozer, "He spoke to the chaos and it became orderly, he spoke to the darkness and it became light!"

To read the account of creation captivates my attention and fills my heart with joy. Simply to know that I serve a God who holds everything in the palm of his hand. I can see the first sunrise as the host of heaven stands on the edge of eternity gazing to the east as God the Father and the Son proclaim the plan of salvation for a race of people not yet fallen. I can smell the fresh dew on the trees, grass, and herbs as the sunlight hits them for the first time. The drops of dew glisten as the sun streaks over the horizon. the silence of eternity breaks forth with birds singing from the trees. I can hear the voice as of a mighty rushing wind as The King of Glory proclaimed, "it was very good!" Gen 1:31.

What a day! What excitement must have rushed through the halls of Glory as the angels, who knew not what the future held, whispered among themselves and watched in amazement at the handy work of the Lord. Just when they thought He was finished, the Lord himself descended from the Sides of the North to dip his hand in the earth and began to form man in his own image. What was this plan? Who was this "man"? The angels must have looked to each other as the stood, petrified, eyes wide and mouth gaping as the Lord begins to form Adam from the dust of the ground.

***

And the LORD God formed man of the dust of the ground, and breathed into his nostrils the breath of life; and man became a living soul. - Genesis 2:7

***

Coffee with our Creator

A daily devotional for God's people. Each day has a scripture from the Old Testament as we discover our Creator each morning and see what the Old Testament scriptures hold for us. We will see glimpses of our Lord and Savior Jesus Christ along with some simple, down to earth help and words of encouragement.

From Glory to Glory

A study of the Word of God to understand the true meaning of God's Glory from the foundation of the world until now. Our Lord said himself as recorded in the Gospel of John 17:22, *"And the glory which thou gavest me I have given them; that they may be one, even as we are one:"*

We as Christians are missing the key ingredient found in this passage. We will explore not only the origin and the meaning but also how to apply these truths to our everyday lives and worship.

www.ingramcontent.com/pod-product-compliance
Lightning Source LLC
Chambersburg PA
CBHW071607040426
42452CB00008B/1274